TO TIMBUKTU
& BEYOND:

A Guide to Getting Started in Missions

Published by William Carey Library
1605 E. Elizabeth Street
Pasadena, CA 91104
www.missionbooks.org

Naomi Bradley McSwain, editorial manager
Johanna Deming and Rose Lee-Norman, assistant editors
Hugh Pindur, graphic design

William Carey Library is a ministry of the
U.S. Center for World Mission
Pasadena, CA | www.uscwm.org

Printed in the United States of America
13 12 11 10 09   5 4 3 2 1 CH

Library of Congress Cataloging-in-Publication Data

Woodard, Marsha.
  To Timbuktu and beyond : a guide to getting started in missions / Marsha Woodard.
       p. cm.
  Includes bibliographical references (p.   ).
  ISBN 978-0-87808-015-1
  1. Missionaries--Appointment, call, and election. 2. Missionaries--Training of. I. Title.

TO TIMBUKTU
& BEYOND:
A Guide to Getting Started in Missions

MARSHA
WOODARD

WILLIAM CAREY
LIBRARY

dedication

To Pastor Pete Beck, Jr., and his gracious wife Jane.
For helping me come in out of the world.
And for starting me on my way to the ends of the earth.

To the remaining unreached people groups:
May you have the chance to hear the Good News of Jesus Christ!

acknowledgements

I am grateful to the missionaries and leaders who have been an example to me. Your lives are woven into every chapter. Thanks to those who freely shared their stories and insights as a background to this book. (Because many of them work in restricted access nations, they will remain anonymous.) A special thanks to Reona Joly, Gloria Cotten, and Anke Tissingh for mentoring me, encouraging me, and championing my efforts.

Thank you to Dr. Bonnie Libby, Dr. Christina Shenvi, Dr. Rick Brown, and Mrs. Kathy Warren for their sacrifice of time to read and edit the manuscript, and for their helpful suggestions.

I am indebted to the members of my church and other friends and supporters for upholding me on the mission field for 26 years. To my faithful prayer partners—thank you for continually presenting this book to God. You know who you are!

Thanks to all who have helped me along the way in my life journey, and above all, to our loving heavenly Father, who has graciously sustained me in His work.

contents

TO TIMBUKTU AND BEYOND

A PROLOGUE

In English, **Timbuktu** has become a metaphor for remote and inaccessible locations. However, Timbuktu is a real place with real people. Like much of the world's population,[1] few of Timbuktu's residents have had the opportunity to hear the Gospel. There is no established church, and little scripture is available in their languages. Across the 10/40 Window[2] millions of people, representing thousands of ethnic groups and languages, are still waiting to hear the message of hope.

While the task may seem daunting, the Church is not sitting still! Each year hundreds of Christians are joining the vast force of cross-cultural missionaries flung around the globe. Thousands more are praying at home for their success. Young people, those in mid-life seeking fresh direction, retirees—all around the world, God's people are choosing to become involved in His purposes for the nations. Particularly exciting is the unprecedented number of missionaries going out from Latin America, Asia and Africa, traditionally "receiving nations" for missions.

---

1   Approximately one-third of the world's population lives areas yet to be penetrated by the Gospel. *Perspectives Exposure*, p. 58.

2   A large geographical area in the Eastern Hemisphere extending between the latitudes 10° to 40° north. The vast majority of the world's unevangelized population lives within this bloc of northern Africa, the Middle East, and Asia.

If you are reading this book, it is probably because, in one way or another, you want to find your place in God's global plan. Congratulations! *Missions is the most fulfilling career path you could possibly embark on—not to mention an incredible adventure!* My hope is that this book will help you in preparation for your journey, because what you do before you go will have a significant impact on your future success.

Before we begin, however, I'd like to share some sobering statistics: *Almost one third of all those heading into long-term cross-cultural missions do not even finish their first term on the field.*[3] The data on why they leave are even more disturbing: lack of a clear call, lack of support from home, interpersonal issues, failed expectations, inability to adapt to a new culture—in all, "preventable reasons" account for about 70% of the missionaries leaving the field. What we don't often realize is that each and every one of these cases is far more than a "statistic" of one less worker. Their leaving brings in its wake far-reaching and often tragic ripple effects.

In my nearly three decades in missions, I've personally known dozens of workers who have left the field pre-maturely. In fact, in my early years, I was once one of them, called home by my church leadership. I can tell you that these missionaries often struggle with a deep sense of failure, sometimes with bitterness, and, more often than not, immobilized from ever returning to the field in the future. The churches that sent them, particularly when it was their first missionary, may be reluctant to invest again in world missions. The team who were left behind on the field also experiences disappointment, and, having spent valuable time and resources to orient the new workers, may balk at the idea of receiving other new members. Finally, Christ's reputation may have been damaged by negative attitudes or cultural faux pas. Every time

---

3   Taylor, p. 125.

a missionary leaves the field before completing his term, progress in our urgent global task takes a severe hit.

So what can we do? Isn't it our goal to get as many laborers as possible out to the harvest field? Yes.... and no. In our zeal to go and to send, we have often neglected critical elements in missionary preparation. *The process of preparation needs to begin long before the official training program, and needs to continue afterwards*, at least through the worker's first term. Missions training programs, even excellent ones, are simply not enough to ensure success on the field. The local church, the missionaries themselves, family and friends, the mission organization, and the field team all have vital roles in this process.

So what is this book all about? It's intended as a guide to help you, your church, and your missions agency identify some of the key steps in getting ready to go into missions. My desire is that it will help you successfully complete your commission, whether God is calling you for two months, two years, or a lifetime of labor in the harvest. Some of the tasks covered seem quite mundane; others involve serious Biblical principles. All are important. In our haste to go or send, let's be careful not to skip over any elements essential to a victorious experience. *My prayer is that as you study, "The Great Shepherd of the sheep will equip you with everything good for doing His will."* [4]

---

4   Heb. 13:20-21.

How to Use This Book

HOW TO USE THIS BOOK

AN INTRODUCTION

"How can I know if I'm called to missions?" "I'm longing to go into missions, but my pastor wants me to work here in the church. What should I do?" "Why did you choose the missions agency you did?" "Do you think we should sell our house, or rent it?" "What about my college debt?" "What should I pack?" "What's the most difficult aspect of being a single woman on the mission field?"

Over the years, I've answered these and dozens of other questions from people much like you who are considering missions. Perhaps some of these same questions have been piling up in your mind, and rumbling around to the point of overwhelming you. Or, like many, maybe you don't even know what to ask! Either way, I hope that this book will serve as **a practical, step-by-step guide for those getting ready to go into full-time missions.** We'll begin with the basic question of knowing and confirming your calling, work through the various steps of preparation, training, and logistics, and carry you through your first few months on the field. Each chapter has a series of tasks for you to prayerfully complete.

Before proceeding, let's agree on a definition of **"missionary"**. While we would certainly recognize many important and God-given ministries within the church, for the purposes of this book, we will limit the term missionary to the following: **an individual who carries the Gospel across cultural, geographical, and/or linguistic boundaries.** Our definition includes those directly involved in church planting, evangelism or Bible translation; those who are "tentmakers" (for example, those who hold secular jobs as a means of entering restricted-access countries[1]); those who express Christ's love through relief and development work, medicine, education, etc.; and those often slighted but absolutely essential support workers—accountants, mechanics, computer experts, and so on—who are also part of a cross-cultural team. Although this book is geared for those who will actually live in another nation or culture, those preparing for short-term trips may find some of the chapters to be useful.

Of course, potential missionaries aren't the only ones who should read this book. *It's also important for those helping to send them*[2]— pastors and church leaders, family, close friends, prayer groups—*and for those who will be receiving them*—mission organizations, training agencies, and field teams. Whether you are a first-time missionary or an experienced worker moving on to a new field, it is intended as a helpful resource to ensure a successful cross-cultural transplant.[3]

---

1   Restricted access countries are nations where open Christian evangelism or church planting would be prohibited for religious or political reasons. Some express their "can do" attitude by referring to them as "CAN"—creative access countries.

2   For a more in-depth look at being a "sender", I highly recommend *Serving as Senders*, by Neal Pirolo. Pirolo provides helpful insights into the needs of missionaries, and specific ways that the home team—whether pastors, mission committee, or friends—can get involved.

3   Let me take a moment to state what this book is *not*. First, it is not an outline for field training programs. Rather it is a guide to the preparation that needs to take place *outside* of most official training programs (although we will briefly discuss what training components an individual may want to select as part of his or her preparation). Second, it is not a manual on the discipleship process—that is the realm of the local church. Finally, it does not pretend to be a theological treatise on missiology or on the nature of a missionary. There are plenty of excellent books available on these topics! In contrast, I have striven to keep the material as simple and practical as possible, while of course endeavoring to align any principles and practices with God's Word and His standards for godly character.

As mentioned above, those of you actually preparing for missions will have a list of assignments to complete as you work through the book. Pastors, friends, receiving organizations: each of you will have a role to play in helping the new missionary along the way. In general, the assignments represent areas of preparation that should be completed in chronological order, although some may be worked on simultaneously. If you have already begun the process of getting ready to go, you may have already completed some of the tasks, so not every chapter will apply to you. Feel free to browse and study the sections that would be helpful at the moment. A note of caution: if you are just getting started in missions, I strongly recommend that you prayerfully complete every assignment listed in the book! Don't become another casualty statistic through pride or haste.

Please don't approach this book as a "to-do" list to mark off as quickly as possible. As you work on each section, take time to consider all that the Lord wants to establish in your life and ministry. Even the most mundane tasks should be accomplished prayerfully, with the guidance of the Holy Spirit. Involve your church leadership and friends in the process. They are a key part of your team. If you are married, be sure to work through each section with your spouse. If you have older children or teenagers, have them join in as well, so that they understand God's purpose in their lives. This will lay a foundation for the kind of partnership you will need on the field.

A final word of encouragement: Remember that **God** is never in a hurry—Peter spent about three years in his training with Jesus; Paul had about ten years in preparation; Joseph spent thirteen years as a slave and prisoner; and Moses was eighty years old when he entered his ministry! I trust that working through this book will enrich your life as you enjoy getting to know God, yourself, your family, and your leaders along the way. ***Now may God bless you as you prepare to embark on an incredible adventure!***

SAND OR BRICKS?
BUILDING A STRONG FOUNDATION

CHAPTER ONE

With my head down against the wind of a Saharan sandstorm, I struggled to make my way back to my one-room "home"—a small cubicle with a concrete floor, a plastic woven carpet, a thin mattress, and a bucket for my personal "necessities". My host family in the big house next door was far from gracious, the food was atrocious, the hygiene worse, I couldn't seem to make any progress in my language study, and above all I felt isolated and lonely. ***"What in the world am I doing here, anyway??"*** I asked myself.

Talk to any veteran missionary. Most will have exciting stories to share of triumph and joy, grand adventures, and touching moments. But they will also remember the hard times, times when they thought about packing up and going home. In these moments, we must have an unshakeable conviction that we really are supposed to be there. We must know that God has called us. Our human strength and determination will simply not be enough to sustain us. In fact, lack of a clear call was found to be one of the top reasons for missionaries returning home before finishing their first term.[1] It is essential to have a solid understanding of what God's Word says about the nations, as well as a clear knowledge of God's personal call and direction in our lives.

---

1   Taylor, p. 94

DEVELOP A GLOBAL VISION

When desert sands blow, whether literally or figuratively, you'll need the assurance that God really is in this "missions thing". *A clear Biblical understanding of God's heart for the nations and a palpable burden for the lost will keep you standing firm even in the fiercest storm.* What does *God* say about the nations? What is on *His* heart? Sadly, very few new missionaries start out with a clear understanding of what God's Word says about reaching the nations. Long-term missionary and teacher Elizabeth Goldsmith tells of a survey taken of people with a strong interest in missions:

> Among the questions asked was, 'How did you first become interested in overseas missions?' I was surprised to learn that not one had replied that their vision came from the Bible. Most had started to support mission through personal interest in someone who had gone overseas. Some had a particular interest in another country. *But not one had said their vision came through study of the Scriptures.*[2] [Emphasis mine]

What about *you*? When asked what the Bible says about missions, are you able to go beyond the "Great Commission"?[3] Before building a house, ensure you have a firm Biblical foundation. As you dig into the Word and experience God's passion for the nations, you will be better prepared to resist the devil and stand firm in the trials that every missionary faces.

How can you go about building a global vision? First, read your Bible with a new eye. In your daily reading or devotionals, note everything

---

2   Goldsmith, p. 61.

3   Matt. 28:19.

that God says about nations and peoples (often translated "Gentiles"), as well as about the lost. Take time to do a word study. It's compelling! From Genesis—when God's covenant people are called to be a blessing to the nations[4]—right through to Revelation—where we witness people from every nation, tribe, people, and language worshipping before the throne of the Lamb[5]—God reveals His longing for the peoples of the earth to know and worship Him.

Virtually every book in the Bible has something to say about the nations. Appendix A lists just some of the related passages.[6] Arm yourself with resources that will guide you in your search of the Scriptures.[7] Do an in-depth study of the book of Acts; observe God's passion reflected in His servant Paul. Keep a journal of all that you discover. Perhaps you can find a study partner who would like to share your journey. I guarantee that God will enlighten your heart as you search out what He has to say.

Second, work to develop "harvest eyesight". Jesus commanded us to "open [our] eyes and look at the fields".[8] Let's face it—most of us have bad eyesight! Our fleshly human nature has us focusing on our own needs, or at best, those of the people around us. You'll need to take deliberate actions to re-focus your vision. It will take time and

---

4   Gen. 12:2-3.

5   Rev. 5:9; 7:9.

6   I am grateful to Southern Nazarene University's excellent website on missions. http://home.snu.edu/~hculbert/biblical.htm.

7   *Let the Nations Be Glad*, by John Piper, gives a excellent theological perspective on "why missions?" A down-to-earth overview of missions is provided in *Catch the Vision 2000*, by Bill and Amy Stearns, and in *Perspectives Exposure: Discovering God's Heart for All Nations and Our Part in His Plan*, edited by Meg Crossman. *Perspectives on the World Christian* Movement, edited by Ralph Winter and Steven Hawthorne, is a thorough study guide to every aspect of missions. Perspectives seminars may be offered in your local area. These are just a few examples of excellent resources that are available.

8   John 4:35.

discipline, but the change will be permanent. Begin with prayer, asking God to give you His heart and His way of looking at the world around you. Then actively turn your eyes outward to what's going on in your city, country, and the nations.

Most Christians, even those with a heart for missions, are only dimly aware of the enormity of the task of world evangelization. I recently taught at a missions training school, and the students were absolutely staggered by the disparity between need and willing workers. Again and again they asked me to put the charts up on the projector, as they simply could not believe the statistics.[9] A few facts to ponder:

- There are still approximately 10,000 distinct people groups that do not have a significant Christian witness in their midst.[10]

- Of the approximately 7,000 languages in the world, only about 400 have an adequate Bible in their mother tongue.[11]

- Half of all non-Christians in the world live in areas where it is highly unlikely for them to hear the Gospel even once. These account for *one third of the world's population!*

- Yet only about one quarter of missionaries work among these difficult-to-reach groups. Ralph Winter calls this "the great imbalance".[12]

---

9   For more in-depth information, see *Perspectives Exposure: Discovering God's Heart for All Nations and Our Part in His Plan*, or *Perspectives on the World Christian Movement*.

10   An unreached people group is an ethnic group among which there is no indigenous community of believing Christians with adequate numbers and resources to evangelize this people group. Exact numbers of groups vary slightly with the precise percentages and criteria used, and are changing as more research is done and the task is accomplished. For up-to-date statistics, I recommend the Joshua Project website: http://www.joshuaproject.net.

11   From Wycliffe Bible Translators, http://www.wycliffe.org/wbt-usa/trangoal.htm.

12   From "Finishing the Task: The Unreached Peoples Challenge", by Ralph D. Winter and Bruce A. Koch, *Perspectives: The Notebook*, p. 249.

These figures are reflected in the chart below. The left side of the graph represents areas that are "reached"—that is, regions where individuals will have a chance to hear and respond to the Gospel message; the right side represents unreached areas, where the population will probably not have a chance to hear the Good News.

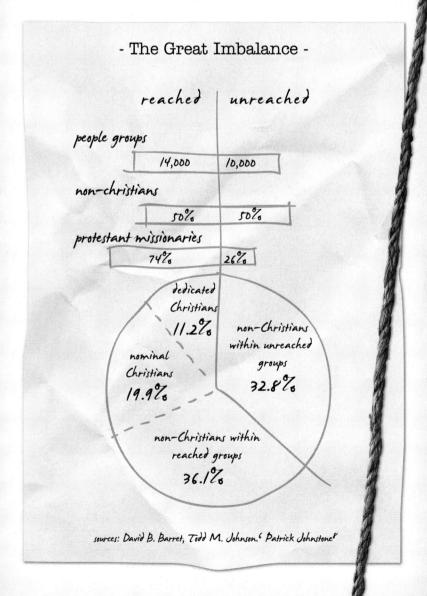

- The Great Imbalance -

	reached	unreached
people groups	14,000	10,000
non-christians	50%	50%
protestant missionaries	74%	26%

dedicated Christians **11.2%**

non-Christians within unreached groups **32.8%**

nominal Christians **19.9%**

non-Christians within reached groups **36.1%**

sources: David B. Barret, Todd M. Johnson.[c] Patrick Johnstone[P]

- Dividing the Resources -

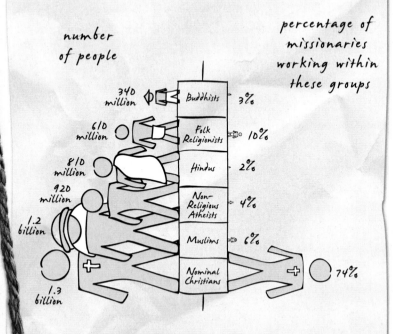

number
of people

percentage of
missionaries
working within
these groups

340 million — Buddhists — 3%

610 million — Folk Religionists — 10%

810 million — Hindus — 2%

920 million — Non-Religious Atheists — 4%

1.2 billion — Muslims — 6%

1.3 billion — Nominal Christians — 74%

IN GOD's WORLD

Christians are allocating only 1.2% of their mission funding to the 1.6 billion people in live in the least-evangelized world.

Only 1% of the Scripture distributions is directed toward the least-evangelized world.

Only 10% of all foreign missionaries and 6% of the full-time Christian workers are directed toward the least-evangelized world.

The chart "Dividing the Resources" should help you grasp this huge disparity.[13] The figures on the left side of the chart show relative proportion of the population in each religious block. The right side shows the proportion of missionaries. Take a moment to think about it. Pray to the Lord of the Harvest to send forth workers into His harvest field[14] and consider what He wants *your* part to be.

We need to maintain and increase our global vision by continually lifting up our eyes to the harvest. There are many practical ways to do so. I've listed a number that have worked for me, but feel free to be creative. Start with two or three ideas that seem comfortable to you, and just get started! Personally, I recommend that *all* Christians, whether headed for missions or not, choose at least a few of these ideas. As you pursue your journey in missions, try to be a catalyst among those around you to "think globally".

Here are some practical ideas for increasing your passion for the nations. Choose 2 or 3 and get started:

- As you read through the Bible, highlight what God says about people, nations, Gentiles, the Kingdom of God, going, being sent, etc. You can also use a concordance to conduct a word study. Appendix A will help you begin a topical Bible study.

- Take five to ten minutes every day to read or listen to world news events. Find one or two countries on a map. Then take a few moments to pray for the situations in the news.

- Use *Operation World*, Praying Through the 10-40 Window, and other prayer guides to pray for different nations.

---

13 *Perspectives Exposure*, p. 102.

14 Matt. 9:37-38.

- Jesus tells us that our heart will follow our treasure,[15] so begin to give to a creditable mission project or missionary.

- Read books or attend seminars on the Biblical basis for missions.

- Participate in missions conferences or visit churches when missionaries are sharing.

- See if a Perspectives on World Missions, Kairos, or other seminar is offered in your community and join up.

- Read missionary biographies. (A great book to start with is with From Here to Irian Jaya, a compilation of biographical sketches from the Apostle Paul to the 20th century.)

- Join a missions prayer group.

- If you already have a burden for a particular nation or group, do some research to find out more about their spiritual needs.[16] Based on what you discover, intercede for the people.

- In our cosmopolitan society, even the smallest towns now have a sizable immigrant population. If you live near a university, there are probably students from dozens of nations right in your own backyard. Build friendships; begin to learn about other cultures first-hand; learn to share the Gospel with people of other backgrounds.

- Take short-term missions trips as often as you can. More than any other way, traveling abroad will excite you for the nations and help you know if God is leading you to cross-cultural work.

---

15 Matt. 6:21.

16 The Adopt-a-People-Group Clearing House (http://www.adoptapeople.com) and the Joshua Project (http://www.joshuaproject.net) have data and profiles on hundreds of unreached peoples.

- Contact missionaries that you know, or workers in an area that interests you. Ask them about their work, their lifestyle, and their needs. When they are visiting, offer hospitality. Begin to pray for them regularly.

- Help develop a missions-focus weekend or group in your own church.[17]

As you are faithful to act on these suggestions, God will stir your heart in ways you never imagined! You will discover particular burdens and desires being ignited in your heart. It is often through these desires that God guides us. My friends Steve and Debbie heard an impassioned sermon about the need for workers in Africa. They had not realized that large populations had never had the chance to hear the Gospel. Their decision was immediate: "Lord, we'll go, if you can use us." That was more than twenty years ago and this humble couple has since been greatly used by God in a number of nations.

God can continue to move us in this same way throughout our lifetime. I had already been serving overseas for a number of years when God began to lift my eyes to a new harvest field. Years ago our team in Latin America had "adopted" a desert people group. For several years I prayed for them—quite frankly, more out of obedience than with passion or zeal. To my surprise, God began to break my heart for this oppressed people. I ended up becoming an answer to my own prayers, first by becoming a true prayer advocate, later going to live among the people, and eventually serving as a coach and trainer equipping others to go.

Specific guidance will come more easily as your heart and mind become more and more aligned with God's passion for the nations. God speaks more clearly when we care about the things that He cares

---

17 Downloadable presentations are available through the Joshua Project. *Catch the Vision 2000* is packed with ideas to maintain your own vision and with resources to share with the church (chapter 13).

about, and when we begin to take steps of obedience, however small. So step out. Begin to pray. Choose some of the ideas above and turn them into habits. Make keeping a global vision a life-long priority! Once you have renewed your harvest eyesight, you can begin to explore more deeply the issue of God's calling and guidance, and in particular, the question that may be stirring in your heart, "How do I know if *I'm* called to go?"

BEFORE MOVING ON

Have you asked God to give you His heart for the nations?

Have you begun an in-depth Bible study concerning God's plan for the nations?

Have you chosen at least two activities to improve your harvest eyesight?

Have you begun to participate in the global task through prayer and giving?

TO GO OR NOT TO GO?
HOW DO I KNOW IF I AM CALLED
TO MISSIONS?

CHAPTER TWO

Is that really You, God? Loren Cunningham, founder of Youth With A Mission ("YWAM") posed this question fifty years ago as he sought to hear and follow God's will for his life.[1] And of course this question still remains *our* starting point in missions. *"Is God calling me to missions?"* At one level, of course, *all believers* have a part to play in taking the Good News to every nation. Pastor and author John Piper states it this way: "There are three possibilities with the Great Commission. You can go. You can send. Or you can be disobedient. Ignoring the cause is not a Christian option."[2] Not everyone is called to "go"—praise God for those who help to send through prayers, finances, helps, and encouragement! (We'll learn more about their important role in chapters 7 and 8).

But there's a good chance that you have picked up this book because you sense you are supposed to be a "go-er"—to leave home and to cross cultural and geographical boundaries. Are you asking yourself (and God) some of these questions: *Do I have a life-time vocational call*

---

1   *Is That Really You, God? Hearing the Voice of God*, by Loren Cunningham with Janice Rogers.

2   *Brothers, We are not Professionals: A Plea to Pastors for Radical Ministry*, by John Piper, p. 187.

like the Apostle Paul,[3] or is it a short-term call? Where am I supposed to go? When? How? Or am I supposed to go at all?

SEEK GOD FOR SPECIFIC DIRECTION

Some of you may feel overwhelmed by the word *"call"*. You may be wondering, **Do I have to decide now what I'm going to do for the rest of my life?** The decision may seem so huge that you can become immobilized by the seeming weight of it. For many of us older missionaries, a traditional "call to missions" was indeed seen as a lifelong one. My experience is an example: As a young child I was fascinated by the mission presentations in our church. I wanted to go to Africa! In my childlike simplicity, I simply understood that I wanted to be a missionary when I grew up; I continued to look towards that goal throughout my teenage years. Despite rebellion in my university years, God was faithful to renew and heighten the call almost immediately after I recommitted my life to Him. That was back in 1979, and missions has been my "career" or "life vocation" ever since.

Nowadays, though, with such rapid changes in technology, political geography and social systems, new missionaries, particularly the younger generation, are reluctant to make such long-term commitments. **Most new workers want to try things out**, to commit for a limited time period or to a specific project.[4] Exploration is healthy, provided you are serious in your commitment of obedience to Christ Himself. Rather

---

3   Acts 26:16.

4   Kath Donovan and Ruth Myors' article, "Reflections on Attrition in Career Missionaries: A Generational Perspective Into the Future" (Taylor, p. 41f) gives excellent insight into the concerns of younger generations. Traditional, older missionaries ("Boosters") believed in a lifetime call to both a country and a mission organization. "Boomers" (age 40 to 60) tend to be project oriented, wanting their time to "count". The younger generation is somewhat insecure concerning the future, and therefore tends to commit for short periods only.

than the question, "Am I called to missions?" we might more fruitfully define our decision-making process as *seeking God's direction for each phase of our lives.*

Whether God calls us to a lifetime vocation or to a short-term commitment, our walk with Him is an on-going cycle of seeking, hearing, and obeying. Don't allow yourself to become "stuck", thinking that you have to make a decision now concerning the rest of your life. God is faithful to unfold our path for us one step at a time; we don't have to know where we'll be ten years down the road. You can begin by taking some trial steps. For example, start out by taking a short-term missions trip with your church. Visit some missionaries you know. Take a missions course that has a cross-cultural outreach. Volunteer to help out in an overseas project for a few months. The key point is to begin to obey God as He directs you.

So how do we "hear" God's voice directing us? Another common cause of paralysis is waiting for a dramatic, supernatural sign from God. An old missionary joke describes a man wanting to know if he's called to China: "I'll know it's You, God, if an airline ticket blows in through the window." I've had some pretty dramatic supernatural experiences during my lifetime, but most of the time, "hearing God" has come through His Word or as the Holy Spirit touches my heart in prayer.

If you're making an important decision in your life, God wants to be involved and will be faithful to direct your path. In fact, God makes it clear that *He delights in communicating with His people.* He promises us that we can know His voice[5] and that He will direct our steps.[6] Open your Bible to just about anywhere in the Old and New Testaments and you can find examples of God communicating with His people.

---

5   John 10:27.

6   Prov.16:9; 20:24, Ps. 37:23.

He spoke with Abraham and Moses "as a man speaks to his friends".[7] He spoke through His prophets. He inspired David and others with songs, poems and wisdom. When a little more drama was called for, He communicated through dreams, visions, angels, miraculous signs, and, on occasion, appeared Himself.[8] In one case of outright rebellion, He even spoke through a donkey![9] And of course He gave us His Son, the Word of God, the perfect model and teacher. ***Bottom line? Trust that God will speak to*** you!

How does God speak to us today? If hearing God is new territory for you, perhaps a few guiding principles will be helpful:

1) His Word. The Bible is a marvelous source of counsel and direction. It is full of wisdom, and is safe, secure, and unwavering. Through our study and meditation of the Word, we can learn and store up sure principles that will keep us steady throughout our life. We are told that the Word will make the simple wise,[10] be a light for our path,[11] equip us,[12] and keep us from straying.[13] Sometimes God will speak through the Word in a special way by highlighting, or "bringing alive", a scripture verse, and showing us how to apply it in a particular situation. If you have not developed a daily habit of feasting on the Word, begin now! It is the safest way to hear from God.

2) His Spirit within us. If you are born again, God's Spirit dwells within you. As you spend time with God, His Spirit will stir emotions, inspire prayers, and gently turn you in new directions. God's peace—or

---

7   Ex.33:11; Jas. 2:23.

8   Gen. 18.

9   Num. 22:28.

10   Ps. 19:7.

11   Ps. 119:105.

12   2 Tim. 3:16-17.

13   Ps. 119:9.

lack of it—is another way we can know if God is speaking to us.[14] This doesn't mean that everything will go smoothly, or even that our emotions will be calm; it's an inner knowing that He is with you and affirming your plans. God often speaks to us through a *desire* for a people group, place, or project. God has promised to give us the desires of our heart *when we delight ourselves in Him*[15]. There is nothing wrong with being led by desires, provided that our other confirmations line up, and that the desire is God-birthed, not carnal. Even in the times when God has called me to extremely difficult places, He has been faithful to fan into flame a passion in my heart for the people He was calling me to.

When God was directing me to join a project located on Spain's southern coast, I was worried because the assignment seemed too good to be true. The location, the culture, the task—everything made it the dream job. Wasn't I supposed to be *sacrificing* for God? God taught me a life lesson as I prayed through my doubts. Why should I be surprised that He would want to bless me?

Of course, the reverse is true as well. If you *don't* feel God's peace, if your emotions are flat, or if you have doubts or dread that just won't go away, consider it a yellow light. Take time out to pray and ask for counsel. You may have natural fears as you face the unknown, or even be experiencing spiritual opposition from our adversary the devil. But it's also possible that the Holy Spirit is trying to re-direct you. Although Paul would later see churches planted throughout Asia, on his first trip to the region, the Spirit of Jesus would not allow them to preach the Word there.[16] I've often wondered just *how* Paul knew this.

---

14   Col. 3:15; Philip. 4:7.

15   Ps.37:4.

16   Acts 16:6-7.

On one occasion I had made a commitment to a particular project in the Arab world—I told the team when I would arrive and announced my plans in my newsletter. However, as the date drew near, nagging inner doubts grew stronger and stronger. I requested prayer and met with my pastor. In the end, I cancelled my plans. It was humiliating to share with my supporters, and even more so when the team leaders wrote scathing letters to my leaders about my so-called lack of commitment. But I knew I had to obey the voice of the Spirit. Soon enough the reason became apparent: right at the time I would have been traveling, the terrorist events of September 11, 2001 took place. The team actually had to turn away all Americans away for security reasons!

3) **Godly people.** God never intended us to hear Him all by ourselves. He has given us leaders and other wise people to help guide us. The Bible, in fact, commands us to listen to these folks. Go to them for advice, asking God in advance to use them, and to prepare your heart to hear what they have to say. Ask them how *they* perceive your gifts and calling, as well as God's timing for any ministry.

God, of course, is God, and He may indeed choose to speak to you in more dramatic or supernatural ways. We must never limit Him, but rather take confidence in His commitment to lead us. More than likely, God has already been speaking to you through His Word, by His Spirit as you pray, or through the people around you. You may have begun to sense a growing inner conviction concerning the nations, a particular location or people, or a special need.

4) **Circumstances.** Both relationships and opportunities to serve can be a way of God pointing us in a new direction. After all, He arranged for us to meet those people and to hear about needs that we can help meet. Prayerfully consider doors that open to you. On the other hand, we want to be careful not to allow negative circumstances to dissuade us from God's purposes. After all, Paul endured financial hardships,

beatings, imprisonments, a shipwreck, and even opposition from other Christians.[17] Was he referring to some of these difficulties when he states that Satan stopped him from carrying out some of his plans?[18]

No matter how God chooses to reveal His will to you, *it is essential that you respond to God's leading by responding in obedience.* Perhaps this will be some small action, such as committing to pray for a people group, or gathering information from a mission organization. Perhaps it will require a greater step of faith, such as declaring yourself willing to "go" and beginning to make plans. Whatever you feel God is asking you to do, begin to act on it. We can't expect God to give us fresh direction if we haven't obeyed what He has already shown us.

Lifelong missionary Thomas Hale sums it up well when he cautions that we can become immobilized by waiting for some "special experience": "Just keep moving as far ahead as you can see. God will reveal the route as you have need." Hale is careful to remind us that we can't expect God to lead us if we are unwilling to actively seek His will, or if we are not willing to obey whatever He may direct us to do.[19] One saying goes, "God can't steer a parked car." Or, a bit more graphically, "God can't lead a dead horse!" Humbly examine your motives. Do you truly want to serve God? Are you willing to help where help is needed? Are you willing to obey in whatever way God leads? If so, you can expect that He will open doors and direct your path.

---

17   Acts 6:4-10.

18   1 Thess. 2:18.

19   Hale, p. 20-21

STEP 3

CHECK YOUR HEARING

God had spoken to me in a clear vision: I was to study at the Spanish Language Institute in Costa Rica in preparation for work with a fledgling church in the Dominican Republic. I was not accustomed to this kind of dramatic spiritual encounter, but God continued to affirm in my heart that this was my next step—in fact, my *first* step into long-term missions. It would involve quitting my job and storing, selling, or giving away all of my belongings—in short, a major lifestyle change! I needed to be completely sure, so I asked God to confirm His direction in three ways: the blessing of my pastor and elders, the blessing of my father, and through a supernatural prophetic word. Perhaps now that I am more used to listening for God's voice I would not need such a weight of evidence, but I would definitely want more than my own inner hearing.

If you sense that God is directing you, and you begin to move toward definite decisions and plans, ***it's important to get confirmation for what you feel God is speaking to you.*** While some people err on the side of wanting too much confirmation (like the man waiting for the ticket to China to blow in), others rush impulsively into major decisions without receiving counsel from others or testing their thoughts in other ways. This may be a reflection of ignorance or immaturity, but can also reveal a spirit of pride or independence. Check your heart! This kind of independence can get you into a lot of trouble. None of us is infallible in hearing God's voice—that's why He has placed us in a Body.

Just how much confirmation do you need? The answer will depend in part on your personality and decision-making modes. If you tend to be timid and overly cautious, God may be nudging you to step out in faith. If you are naturally impulsive and headstrong like me, God may be saying, "Slow down and pull in the reins!" But *everyone* should seek confirmation for any major, life-changing decisions. In general terms, the greater the effect of your decision on your life (and on your family, if you're married), the more confirmation you need.

Let me give a couple of examples. Suppose your church has organized a ten-day summer work trip to a neighboring country and you'd like to go. Naturally, you'll want to pray, discuss it with your parents or spouse, and run it by your church leaders. However, barring any economic or family difficulties, your decision is not going to cause a major upheaval in your life. On the other hand, imagine that your plans would require a three-year commitment, and would involve re-locating your family to another continent. The ramifications of the move would include quitting your job, selling your home, changing your children's educational plan, and making a major financial investment for language learning and travel expenses. Well, you'll definitely want to be sure that the plan is in God's will and timing!

What are some practical—and Biblical—ways to confirm God's leading? First, any plan must line up with God's Word. Of course, there's plenty of Scriptural backup to encourage you to go "to the uttermost ends of the earth," as you've discovered if you've followed some of the suggestions in chapter 1. But be sure your *specific* decisions and timing line up with *all* of God's Word. Consider Biblical principles concerning money (debt and obligations), family, fulfilling commitments, submission to leaders, etc., etc. I trust that if you are passionate enough to want to go into missions, you desire to please God in *every* area of your life.

Second, never, never, never make an important decision alone. The Book of Proverbs tells us just how important it is to get wise counsel, and conversely, how foolish it is not to. Here is just a sampling of verses:

"The way of a fool seems right to him, but a wise man seeks advice."
(Prov. 12:15)

"Wisdom is found in those who take advice." *(Prov. 13:10)*

"Plans fail for lack of counsel, but with many advisers they succeed."
(Prov. 15:22)

*"Listen to advice and accept instruction, and in the end you will be
wise."* *(Prov. 19:20)*

An obvious place to start is with your family. If you are still single
and living at home, include your parents in your thinking. They know
you better than most people, and desire the best for you. Even as an
adult, you can ask your parents for their input and for a blessing on
your decisions, particularly if they are believers. God will honor our
heart to honor our parents.[20] In my own case, I had already been on my
own for a number of years when I began making plans for missions;
even so, I knew my father's approval would be important. Dad gave
me some wise advice, knowing some of my character flaws, and then
pronounced a blessing. I believe that in doing so, spiritual authority
was imparted in the heavenly realms. Now that Dad has passed away,
I look back on that evening as a cherished memory.

For a few, there may come a point when, like pioneer missionary Jim
Elliott, you will need to obey God rather than your parents. His parents
were distressed at his plans to go to the jungles of South America (where
he was later martyred). Elliott wrote to them:

*I do not wonder that you were saddened at the word of my going to
South America. This is nothing else than what the Lord Jesus warned
us of when He told the disciples that they must become so infatuated*

---

20   Ex. 20:12; Eph. 6:2.

with the kingdom and following Him that all other allegiances must become as though they were not. And He never excluded the family tie... Grieve not, then, if your sons seem to desert you, but rejoice, rather, seeing the will of God done gladly.[21]

Hopefully, your parents will joyfully encourage you on your way. In any case, be sure to listen to and consider all that they have to say.

If you are married, it is essential that you seek the Lord together with your spouse. While this may seem painfully obvious, I've met more than one unfortunate couple who had not made their decisions together. Dragging a reluctant spouse to the mission field is courting personal and family disaster. Many parents also choose to involve their **children** in the decision-making process. The choices you make will obviously have a huge impact on their lives. I am not advocating that children have an equal "vote"; the family is not a "democracy". However, their feelings are important, and they do need to be included in your discussions. Even young children can hear the Lord. If they hear from *Him*, they will eagerly participate in what God desires to accomplish through your family, rather than continually complaining about the move.

Next, talk with your pastor and other church leaders. They are a gift from God, given to protect and care for you, and to help equip you for ministry.[22] If you head out into missions (or make any other major decision) without their approval and blessing, you are removing yourself from under God's umbrella of protection. This principle is so important—and so often tragically ignored—that I have devoted the next chapter to the importance of being sent out by your home church. Everyone needs to be under authority and accountable to church leadership.

---

21 *Shadow of the Almighty: The Life and Testament of Jim Elliot*, by Elisabeth Elliot, p. 132.

22 Heb. 13:17; Eph. 4:11-12.

By the way, friends, family and leaders can often be objective enough to add **common sense** to the equation. It's true that God sometimes calls us to do things that don't make sense, but usually He will guide us into ministries that will use our background, education, experience, gifts and talents. When our zeal outpaces our wisdom, God can use others to bring us back down to earth and point us in the right direction.

At the same time that you are seeking counsel from others, **ask God for confirmation within your own heart.** If you believe that you are called to a particular place or task, pray that God would increase and clarify your vision and desire. During my first internship in the Sahara, I sensed God was directing me to return long-term. I confess I was initially reluctant—it was a *very* hard place—but was willing to do whatever God told me. As I prayed for God to make His will clear, He changed my reluctance to desire, and ultimately to pleading for the chance to serve Him there.

Should you ask the Lord to give you an outward sign? Many people ask for confirmation through circumstances, a special sign, a prophetic word, etc. Signs have often been a source of encouragement in my life, as they were for our doubting friend Gideon,[23] but circumstances should never be our *primary* source of awareness of God's will. Not every open door is the one God wants us to walk through, nor is every closed door a sign that *God* closed the door. Bear in mind that the devil can "masquerade as an angel of light".[24] For this reason I am always cautious with "signs", only allowing them to add to the balance of more sure ways of hearing.

Tests or pretexts? Can we ask for too much confirmation? Sometimes a demand for more "proof" of God's will is a thinly veiled disguise for an unwillingness to obey God. Are you covering up excuses with a

---

23   Judges 6.

24   2 Cor. 7:14.

false spirituality of "waiting to hear God's voice"? Jesus commanded His church to take the Gospel to the very ends of the earth. *Going and sending should be the norm, not the exception, in every local church.* Why are so few going?[25] Here are just some of the reasons I've heard people give:

- I want to finish my education (or get more).

- I need to pay off my college debt.

- I don't want to go to the field single.

- We're newlyweds, and want to take time to build our marriage.

- We have young children, so travel would be difficult.

- We have school-aged children, and education would be a problem.

- We have teen-aged children, and moving now would be emotionally traumatic for them.

- I need to care for my aging parents.

- I'll go when I'm retired.

- I'm too old!

Add concerns about safety, health, finances, leaving family, and various other difficulties, and, well, you've got quite a list of "reasons"! While all of the above are valid concerns, you can see that it would be very easy to put off going into missions almost indefinitely.

---

25 In 2000 there were approximately 200,000 cross-cultural missionaries, for a world population of close to 6.1 billion (*Operation World*, p. 747). Only about one fourth of those missionaries were working within the unreached areas where one third of the world's population resides (*Perspectives Exposure*, p. 67). *That means there is only one missionary for every 40,000 people in frontier regions!* (These numbers are constantly changing; visit the Joshua Project website for up-to-date statistics: http://www.joshuaproject.net.)

Jesus was always clear in His focus: "My food is to do the will of Him who sent me and to finish His work."[26] He was also clear that the harvest had both priority and urgency:

> *Do you not say, 'Four months more and then the harvest'? I tell you, open your eyes and look at the fields! They are ripe for harvest. Even now the reaper draws his wages, even now he harvests the crop for eternal life.*[27]

What about you? Yes, you absolutely need to pray and hear God. But be alert to the dangers of false excuses. The longer you stay at home, the stronger the pull of career, security, and comfort. Culture and our own flesh are potent! Before you know it, years, even a lifetime, have slipped through your hands like so much sand. Begin to actively move towards missions—God is faithful, and will re-direct you or delay you if you're off track. But He will never force you to move. As Hale exhorts, "God can easily stop you. His problem is starting you."[28] Are you ready? In the following chapters we'll begin the preparation process for going.

---

26 John 4:34.

27 John 4:35-26.

28 Hale, p. 21.

BEFORE MOVING ON...

Have you spent time in the Word and in prayer concerning your future plans?

Check your heart. Are you willing to obey whatever God tells you, or have you made excuses?

Have you talked and prayed with your family members?

Have you met with your pastor or other church leaders?

What kinds of confirmation has God given you? Be specific.

Have you obeyed in the small steps God has asked you to take?

AIM FOR GOD'S HIGHEST BLESSING!

CHAPTER THREE

Ana Maria[1] tearfully recounted her interview with her pastor. Things had not gone as she had wished, and she wanted our advice and—she hoped—our intervention. Regrettably, Ana Maria's story was all too common: She had recently attended a dynamic interdenominational mission conference, and her heart was touched as she learned of nations that had never had the opportunity to hear the Good News. Could God be calling **her** to an unreached people group? She felt that He was, and she returned home with excitement about this new direction for her life, ready to begin whatever was necessary to prepare herself for the task.

Unfortunately, her pastor didn't share her enthusiasm. For one thing, her country was accustomed to **receiving** missionaries. Only a handful of cross-cultural missionaries had ever been sent from their nation, and none from her denomination. At that time, most church leaders' evangelistic vision centered on their own nation and denomination. Ana Maria's pastor said there was work to be done at home and in the church. He wanted Ana Maria to remain at home as church secretary and librarian. To complicate matters, both her culture and her denomination tended to embrace a somewhat authoritarian style of leadership. In her pastor's eyes, the case was closed.

---

1   Not her real name.

What counsel would you give Ana Maria? Should she head to the mission field without her pastor's consent? Should she submit to his demands? Or should she leave her church and find another one? The answers are far from simple. I have personally wrestled with this kind of agonizing decision three times: once when I was asked to wait for a year; on another occasion when I was asked to return home from the field; and again when I was asked to relinquish a key part of my ministry. God guided me and comforted me uniquely in each situation; nevertheless the same principles concerning authority and missions applied each time.

Before advising Ana Maria in her situation, let's take a look at *your* situation. How does *your* church leadership feel about your desire to go into missions? Are they working with you? Opposing your plans? Indifferent? Requesting that you wait or get more training? **What you decide about your relationship with your home church will have serious implications for your future and your success or failure on the mission field.**

STEP 4
___

TAKE STEPS TO OBTAIN THE BACKING OF YOUR SPIRITUAL AUTHORITIES

First, let's talk about who and what "spiritual authorities" are. Throughout both the Old and New Testaments we see examples of God-chosen, God-anointed leaders. Some were outstanding leaders; some were not. All of them were human and fallible, yet they had been placed in their positions by God to lead, guide, and protect His people. With those responsibilities came a special relationship with God and divine help for their tasks. What's our role? We are commanded to submit to and honor those in authority. Just a few Scriptural examples are: Parents (Eph. 6:1-2); employers (Eph. 6:5-6); government (Rom. 13:1-2); spiritual leaders (1 Thess. 5:12-13; Heb. 13:17).

The common thread running through all of these Scriptures is that those in authority are given to help and bless us. God's blessing, wisdom, and delegated authority flows through them to us:

- For protection, especially from self-deception.

- For sound advice and wisdom.

- For direction and guidance.

When we honor and obey them, God commands a blessing on us.

Looking at it from the other direction, **what happens if we don't honor and submit to them?** I believe it lessens our safety and security because we are no long receiving this God-ordained help. We also place ourselves in the position of dishonoring God. The book of Numbers has a lot to say about those who grumble against leaders. In fact, it's pretty scary! It seems Israel was constantly challenging the authority of Moses. Some of the consequences were fire from heaven (Chapter 11:1), plague (11:33), and wandering in the desert for an entire generation (14:33-34). When some "well-known community leaders" became "insolent", they were swallowed up in the earth (Chapter 16)! Even Miriam and Aaron wanted equal authority. The result? Miriam ended up leprous, and was only cleansed through Moses' intercession (Chapter 12). God takes His delegated authority very seriously, and so should we. God may not send fire from heaven, but He *will* discipline His children.

But what if I have a bad leader? You think *you've* got problems? Joseph had family who wanted to kill him, and an employer who threw him into prison based on a false accusation. Nevertheless, whether slave, prisoner, or right-hand man to Pharaoh, Joseph honored his superiors in both his attitude and his work. Look at David's situation: his leader, King Saul, was a manic-depressive maniac, so obsessed with killing

David that he followed him around the wilderness with the whole army of Israel! Even though David had already been chosen and anointed by God, Saul was still in power, and David was determined not to dishonor him. When a seemingly golden opportunity came for David to kill him and save himself, he refused to do it: "The Lord forbid I should do such a thing to my master, the Lord's anointed, or lift my hand against him; for he is the anointed of the Lord (1 Sam. 24:6) ." [2]

In the same way, we are responsible to respect and submit to our leaders. (Of course, we are never required to obey a request that is immoral or contrary to God's Word.) God will deal with those who misuse their power, just as He did with Saul. Hopefully none of you will have to undergo such extreme experiences, but one thing is certain: none of your leaders will be perfect, either at home or on the field. God will allow you to be subjected to different kinds of leadership to test your heart towards authority. It's part of our spiritual training, just as it was for David and Joseph.

If you have a pastor who is resistant to you going into missions, or is simply uninterested, you may be tempted to skip over this step and just go on ahead on your own. After all, you have the necessary resources, and you've heard from God, right? While this may be true, before jumping the gun, *let's look at five reasons why having the blessing of local church leadership is so crucial for missionaries.* At the end of the chapter we'll come back to some steps you can take if you have leaders who oppose your plans.

1) Your pastor and leaders can provide wise counsel and protection. The Bible states that our heart is deceitful above all things and beyond cure (Jer. 17:9). We have many blind spots in our lives, and this is why God has surrounded us with experienced and godly people.

---

2   For a more in-depth look at our relationship with authority, read about Saul, David, and Absalom in Gene Edwards' *A Tale of Three Kings.*

Your leaders may see some character or maturity issues that need to be worked on before you're ready to go--only a fool is wise in his own eyes (Prov. 26:12). They will also be a future source of comfort and advice when you're "between a rock and a hard place" on the field.

2) Your church leaders will guide the congregation into becoming full partners in your ministry. As we will discuss in Chapters 7 and 8, your church will play a vital role in your success on the field: prayer back-up, practical helps, financial support, and overall encouragement. Leaving home without this kind of connection and backing (financial and otherwise) can leave you high and dry on the field. The congregation's involvement is essential, so you want the leaders as advocates, not detractors, of your cause.

3) How you relate to your authorities at home is a good indicator of how you will deal with your authorities on the field. If you are struggling with submitting to authority at home, the issue will only be magnified on the field. With the stresses of a new culture, a new ministry assignment, being far from home, and so on, new missionaries frequently feel the need to "vent their frustrations" (a nice way of describing what really happens), and this is usually directed at—you guessed it—their leaders! In pioneer situations those in authority may often have some rough edges. They didn't head out to a remote area because they were pastors, but because they were hard-shelled pioneers. Before you go, ask for God to give you *His* heart and understanding toward authority, and consider your remaining time at home as a "school" to get it right.

4) Being sent out by—and remaining accountable to—local church leadership is a Biblical pattern. As you study the book of Acts, you'll see that Barnabas was sent out by the Jerusalem leaders to help and encourage the new group of believers in Antioch (11:22). He in turn sent for Paul (whom he had earlier introduced to the church

leaders) (11:25; 9:27-28). As the church in Antioch grew, it became a premier "missionary church". Antioch's incredible church planting movement all began with the leaders praying and fasting together, and sending off Paul and Barnabas (13:1-3). After their journey, they returned to the church in Antioch and reported on "all that God had done through them" (14:26-27).

Does this mean that there is no place for parachurch organizations? Not at all! It means that the individual's local church does the *sending*. In my congregation, for example, some of our missionaries work with organizations such as Wycliffe, YWAM, and others; others work with "sister" churches in our network; still others are part of teams working with national leaders. We'll discuss these various team options more in Chapter 5, but the important point is that each worker needs the backing, both spiritual and practical, of his or her home church.

Bottom line? Submission to our church authorities is Biblical. We have a mandate to honor and obey our leaders "so that their work will be a joy and not a burden, for that would be of no advantage to you" (Heb. 13:17). Do you want God's full blessing on your work and ministry? Then do all that is in your power to obtain that blessing through the channel of God's delegated authorities.

Now let's look again at Ana Maria's case—and perhaps your own— and think about some practical steps to take. If you feel that you have heard God concerning missions, but, as in Ana Maria's case, your leaders are resistant to your plan, what are your options? Here's what I would suggest you do:

- **First, humble yourself, and listen carefully to the reasons your leaders give** for opposing your plans. Are they questioning your individual calling? Your particular plans? Your timing? Take to heart their counsel, particularly regarding family and character issues. Be sure that you are not acting in pride or independence.

- If you are still in disagreement, **ask your leaders to pray with you about the issues** for a specific period of time and then talk again. When you pray, don't pray for *your* will, but sincerely open yourself to hear what *God's* will is. If, after this, you are still at an impasse, **continue to pray, and give God time to work in the situation.** God's not in a hurry—He's a master craftsman who wants a perfect work.

- **Seek wise counsel from other mature, godly people** who are close to you. Don't be like Rehoboam, who rejected the advice of the elders, and consulted the young men who were his friends. He lost half of his kingdom as a result (1Kings 12).

- As you wait, **consider that God may want to use you to bring a missions vision to you church.** Review some of the suggestions in chapter one and think about how you can be used at home.

- **If your church leadership is completely resistant to or indifferent to foreign missions *and* you have followed the above steps, then you may need to look for another church** that has a more Biblical vision for the nations. This should be your last step, not your first. *Don't* use it as an excuse to ignore God-given counsel for your life. Avoid independence and self-deception.

- Recognize that if you change churches, it will take time for the new leaders and congregation to get to know you. Take the necessary time to build relationships so that you can be sent out with the full support of your new church.

Ultimately, you are responsible to obey God and give account to Him. This means that you must follow His individual guidance and directives, but at the same time honor the principles He establishes in His Word.

Remember that one of the ways we "hear" God is through the people He places in our lives. If these principles are in seeming conflict, have faith that God is able to resolve them and direct your steps.

I have met many missionaries who have *no* home church. In some cases, the churches that sent them out later dissolved, divided, or discontinued their backing while the workers were overseas, placing the missionaries in an extremely challenging dilemma. Other missionaries simply chose to go independently. In both cases the missionaries were deprived of some of the blessings and protection offered by being backed by a congregation.

If, having followed all the steps above, you feel there is absolutely no way for you to be sent out by a local church, be sure that at least you are part of a team or organization that provides accountability and pastoral care. Please *don't* head out completely independently. The enemy is expert at picking off isolated sheep who are wandering out alone!

To sum up: Your leaders' blessing and backing is important! Do all that **you** *can to make your relationship with them a fruitful one.* Hopefully, they will be willing to get involved with the specifics of your plans. Show them this book and the steps you are working through. Their advice and help will prove invaluable all along the way and will lay the foundation for a healthy on-going working relationship.

One final clarification: Your church may be willing and able to bless you and back you spiritually, but be unable to support you financially. Most missionaries receive their support from a variety of sources, so your home church may not necessarily be your prime base of income. *Don't confuse finances with the principles of blessing discussed above.* However, please encourage your church to get involved with your funding as they are able to so that they become active partners in your ministry.

BEFORE MOVING ON...

Have you shared your heart and vision with your pastor and other church leaders?

Have you prayed that God would speak through them, and sincerely listened to their counsel?

Have you asked them to help you as you work through this book and make specific plans?

If your leaders are opposed to your plans, are you willing to submit to their counsel? If not, do you have a Biblical reason?

Have you given God sufficient time to work in the situation, and sought counsel from other wise and godly people?

WHAT DO YOU MEAN "WAIT"?!

CHAPTER FOUR

My vision was clear: I was called to missions! I had plenty of confirmation: the Biblical call to take the Gospel to every nation, the on-going, strong stirring in my heart, the blessing of my father, prophetic words, and the encouragement of my pastor and elders. We even agreed on *where* I was to go: to Central America for language study and an apprenticeship with a local pastor. I was "psyched" and ready to start packing. However, to my dismay, my leaders asked that I wait for at least another year or two. My heart sank at the decision, but hindsight proved their wisdom. I had a lot of learning and maturing to do.

François and Marie's[1] disappointment was even greater. Their leaders had affirmed them in their plan to work in North Africa, so they had gone ahead and prepared for the transition, actually packing and moving out of their home. Somehow there had been a miscommunication: the leaders didn't mean right away. The couple wanted François and Marie to have further discipleship in the church. The couple graciously submitted to their pastor, although the letdown was keen.

Have your leaders asked **you** *to wait? If you are young, perhaps your parents have. Or maybe you feel God Himself is not opening the door yet.* Or perhaps you've been on the field for a while, but whether due to circumstances or at your leaders' request, you find yourself back home for a year or so. Don't look at this as a frustrating delay. God

---

1   Names and circumstances have been slightly changed.

wants you to thrive and bear good fruit on the field, and He knows exactly what kind of training ground you need. The work God does in your life at home will probably be exactly what you will need on the field. During my waiting period, I received a solid grounding in the Word of God and guidance in developing my ministry gifts. Some important "growing up" took place, as well. So open your heart and cooperate with God's school.

STEP 5

TAKE FULL ADVANTAGE OF YOUR PREPARATION TIME AT HOME

Your attitude toward the waiting period will have a lot to do with whether it turns into a waste of time or a building time. Humble yourself. Open yourself to God, and also to your leaders. Give them permission to speak into your blind spots. They are responsible before God for your well-being, and have a special anointing, ability, and wisdom to hear from Him on your behalf. And remember that ultimately God is the Master Builder! During my initial waiting period, and later during a "time out", I learned some principles that may help you to make the most of this stage in your preparation.

1) To get the most out of waiting, recognize that God is never passive in our lives. He is always at work. Neither should you be passive, but rather actively engaged in learning, growing, and working toward your goals. ***Ask yourself the question, "What needs to happen for me to get to the mission field?"*** More importantly, "What needs to happen for me (and my family) to grow in Christ? Then act on the answers. Stay focused on your goal. This time period is just as important as any kind of formal training, whether theological or missiological. God has particular lessons that He wants to cover. The more you cooperate in the process, the faster you can "graduate".

2) Make a specific list of any areas that God wants to work on. The best way to begin is to ask your leaders and other mature people who know you well. Yes, it will probably be embarrassing, but you can get directly to the issues if you are willing to have people speak frankly into your life. They will also be able to address any "blind spots" in your character or personal development. This is particularly true if your leaders have doubts about your plans or have said "not yet". Ask them why. Also spend time alone with God and ask *Him* to reveal any weak areas in your foundations. Are any of the following true for you?

- Character issues or immaturity.

- Moral issues, addictions, or other persistent struggles in your spiritual walk.

- Interpersonal issues or difficulty relating to others, particularly authority.

- Marriage and family tensions.

- Past hurts or wounds that would cause you to be over-sensitive in a certain area, or any areas of unforgiveness.

- Lack of Biblical training and discipling.

- Lack of ministry experience.

- Lack of educational background or training.[2]

- Debt.

- Not enough time or contact in the church for the leaders and congregation to know you well.

One area we* all *need to work on is developing vibrant, personal devotional times. If you struggle with having a regular quiet time with

---

2   A college degree is not always required. However, some higher education or technical training is always an asset on the field, particularly in so-called "closed" countries, where your means of entry may be your professional capacity (engineer, English teacher, nurse, software specialist, etc.).

the Lord—worship and thanksgiving, prayer, study and meditation of the Word—join the crowd! Probably most of us do, at least some of the time. However, these personal disciplines will be essential to survival, let alone fruitfulness on the field. Particularly in pioneer situations, there may not be a Sunday morning worship service, a mid-week Bible study, a loving pastor, a group of best friends who will speak into your life, and so on. I know in my life there have been times where it's just been me and God and my Bible. Even if you do have excellent support from your field team, you'll need your own intimate time with God. Begin setting aside time and building up your devotional skills. There are plenty of excellent books[3] and resources on this area, so ask for help to get started if you need it.

Of course, we'll never be fully mature, fully healed, or fully trained, but we can and must deal with any major stumbling blocks. Please don't wait until you're overseas to deal with these issues! Most of them are potential trigger points for a "crash and burn". You'll have enough pressure dealing with culture shock, team dynamics[4], and the pressures of ministry. Be transparent with your leaders. You want to go healthy, not just go. God in His mercy gives us the opportunity to get things straight *before* leaving.

3) Work with your pastor or a godly mentor to develop plans and objectives to enhance your growth and overcome any problem areas. Again, be actively engaged. Find a mature, trustworthy person and pray together about how you can work toward your goals. Do you need further training? One-on-one discipleship? Counseling to overcome past hurts? A ministry internship? A financial plan to get

---

3   One of many that I have enjoyed is *Celebration of Discipline: The Path to Spiritual Growth*, by Richard J. Foster.

4   Interpersonal conflicts remain an all too common reason for missionaries leaving the field prematurely. "Missionary Attrition: The ReMAP Research Report", Peter W. Brierley, in Taylor, p. 93.

out of debt? Family counseling? Set up specific goals, strategies, and tentative timetables. Then stay accountable to your leader or mentor on a regular basis. Don't assume it is his or her responsibility to follow through—leaders are usually very busy people. It is your job to stay in touch with them and to set up appointments.

4) Throughout the preparation period, keep your eye on the goal. Always remember the reason for this training period: missions! It is so easy to lapse into passivity, particularly if we are in a rather unpleasant phase of God's discipline in our lives. Write down your vision and all that God has spoken to your heart. Re-read it regularly, and continue to pray for God's release into His purposes for your life. It might be good to periodically look at the list of possible pretexts at the end of chapter 2 and check your heart. It is so easy to get distracted and detoured from missions. This is exactly what the enemy wants. Never give up!

5) Continue to stoke the fires of your global passion. Review the activities in chapter 1 for developing and maintaining your zeal for the nations. In particular, continue to gain experience through short-term trips and local outreaches.

One final word of advice: ***God may be using this time to test your heart.*** Will you stay humble even when you don't get your way? Will you trust in the Lord even when it appears that doors are closing? Will you have faith in God's promises for your life? Sometimes God takes away our outward ministry to test and strengthen the inner man. You may feel that every door has shut, both at home and abroad. Even your sense of God's presence may be temporarily dulled. Many have called this experience ***"death of a vision"***.

Over the years I've passed through this refining process several times. The most difficult was in my younger years when my former pastor abruptly called me back from the field. His letter was strong and unequivocal—I was to come home immediately. A misunderstanding had occurred, and there didn't seem to be much chance of working it out. My obedience to authority was tested to the limit. I returned home, with no open door for the future. The experience was crushing—one of the most difficult in my entire Christian life. Plans, hopes, vision were nullified. I went through life in a horrible kind of numbness. What were the tests? Would I still love and trust God and His goodness? Would I still honor my leaders? Would I continue to walk by faith and believe in His purposes for my life?

Three and a half years later, just as unexpectedly as the charge to come home, God worked supernaturally to change the hearts of my authorities. I was released to return to the field, and within weeks was joyfully working in the harvest. God restored all that had been taken away, and now with a greater portion.

If you are experiencing this kind of valley, and it seems your hopes will not come to pass, dig deep in the Lord. ***Trust that God will bring about that which He has planned and promised for your life. The hotter the refining fire, the greater the gold of faith that will remain.***

BEFORE MOVING ON...

Have you submitted to your leaders timetable for your plans and listened to their concerns?

Have you worked with a mentor to develop a plan for specific areas of growth?

Have you worked through any major hindrances in your life (lack of foundations, relational problems, finances, etc.)?

Have you set goals to develop your personal disciplines of prayer, systematic Bible reading, and meditation?

Are you taking practical steps to maintain your vision for the nations?

Are developing a deeper intimacy with God during your time of testing?

NARROWING THE FIELD—
WHICH ORGANIZATION IS FOR ME?

CHAPTER FIVE

What's your flavor? I once visited a family-owned ice cream stand in Mexico that advertised over 100 flavors. They served all the traditional favorites like chocolate and vanilla, a wide range of luscious tropical fruit flavors, and some downright weird selections, such as "refried beans" and "guacamole" flavors! Similarly, there are hundreds of missions organizations, each with its own distinctive flavor or style—some are quite traditional; some are, well, a little strange; and there is a wonderful variety of everything in between!

For several summers I worked with a multi-agency project in southern Spain distributing literature to North Africans. Each year we received dozens of teams representing a number of denominations and missions organizations. By the third summer, I could make some good predictions about the various groups, and secretly assigned "flavors" to the sponsoring organizations. Teams from organization "X" almost always had excellent leadership and organization, worked cheerfully and diligently, but frequently complained about the food and accommodations at the 2-star hotel. (They were the "vanilla" team.) Teams from organization "Y" were usually younger, a bit less mature, but were willing to do whatever was asked, including working all night or staying in a "no-star" hostel. (The "pineapple/mango" team.) The "pistachio" teams were dedicated, brainy, humorous, and occasionally a little nutty. Together we made a fantastic ice-cream sundae, with each individual team working tightly together.

So what does ice cream have to do with missions? Before joining a team or an organization, you'll want to discover their "flavor". If you are vanilla—traditional, conservative, organized—look for a group with a similar style. You might do fine on a strawberry team, but you'll probably be frustrated on an adventurous, risk-taking pineapple-mango team. You'll be living and working closely with your colleagues, and will be required to agree to the group's policies and regulations, so you'd best find out something about them before signing on board!

STEP 6

CHOOSE THE ORGANIZATION YOU WILL WORK WITH

How do you select the organization you'll work with? In the same way you would choose a spouse or a business partner: *Carefully!* Bill Taylor puts it this way:

> *Remember that joining a mission agency is similar to marriage (though it's not always for life). It's a serious, long-term, mutual commitment with heavy implications. Joining the right "ministry family" means time spent "courting"—getting to know each other, evaluating the fit.... Remember that there are no perfect organizations. Be realistic. Beware of rapid decisions and "love affairs" with a particular team. The post honeymoon blues can be fierce![1]*

There are hundreds, if not thousands, of options out there. *Let's begin by getting a bird's eye view.* Most missionaries will fall into one of the following categories: independent missionaries, those belonging to a denominational mission board, those sent out as part of a local

---

1   Hoke and Taylor, p. 65, 68

church team, and those serving with a parachurch missions organization (such as Wycliffe Bible Translators, Youth With A Mission, Campus Crusade, etc.).

Independent missionaries. Some missionaries shun the idea of joining a team or agency. Unless your church is sending you directly to work with another local church, I would strongly discourage you from going out on your own! The Bible is clear that the minimum team size is two. More is better. A team provides a variety of gifts and talents, as well as mutual edification, accountability, and protection. This is particularly important for newer missionaries, who may be unaccustomed to the kind of spiritual warfare they'll experience, and who will need the cross-cultural wisdom of more experienced workers. If you find yourself reluctant to be part of a team, prayerfully check your reasons. Is it pride? Do you lack of the interpersonal skills needed to work with others?

On a positive note, more and more workers are entering so-called restricted access countries as "tentmakers" (referring to the Apostle Paul's profession[2]). Nevertheless, even if you go this route, do some research and make every effort to connect with a team or national church working in the area where you hope to work.

Denominational mission boards. Many denominations around the world have their own mission agencies. Perhaps your denomination *only* supports missionaries through their own organization. That's fine, as long as you and your pastor feel good about the match. However, I recommend you go ahead and work through the assignments in this chapter, to learn about your own denomination's policies, as well as to learn how others might differ. Understanding how agencies differ will help you get along with other groups you may be cooperating with on the field.

---

2   Acts 18:3.

Local church teams. Again, this is an excellent option for you as long as it is a good match for your calling, gifts and personality. Sometimes individuals are pressured to work in an area (geographical or ministerial) that differs from the way they feel the Lord is leading them. If this is your situation, you'll need to be honest with your church's leadership and ask them about being released into another area. They may want you to work first with their project as a kind of internship or "proving period", in which case you can receive some valuable on-the-field training.

Mission organizations. There is a debate as to whether parachurch organizations are a true Biblical pattern for missions, and sadly, mission agencies have gotten a bad rap in some circles.[3] Yet these institutions have faithfully, and for the most part successfully, deployed hundreds of thousands of cross-cultural workers since modern missions began over two centuries ago![4] Indeed we could make a case that Paul's team on his third missionary journey was a pattern of a parachurch team. Although Paul was sent by the Antioch church, his team members came from a number of different cities and churches. As leader, Paul established the direction for the team and made "personnel" decisions without supervision from the home church.[5]

Many of mission organizations have decades of experience which enables them to offer an expertise that most local churches are simply not equipped to provide, for example: language learning methods,

---

3   Patrick Johnstone provides an in-depth theological and practical analysis of the interdependency of the local church, mission agencies, and training institutes (seminaries and Bible colleges). See Johnstone, *The Church is Bigger than You Think,* chapters 13 to 19

4   Indeed, the pioneers of modern missions, including William Carey and Hudson Taylor, generally formed missionary "societies". Carey worked with The Baptist Missionary Society; Taylor established the China Inland Mission. Other early pioneering agencies including Africa Inland Mission (AIM), Sudan Interior Mission (SIM), and Heart of Africa Mission (now WEC). See Johnstone, Ibid., chapter 8.

5   See especially Acts 20:4-6.

cross-cultural adaptation, contextualized evangelism, area-specific expertise (Islam, China, relief and development, etc). Until a church is fully equipped in cross-cultural missions, it should warmly embrace a partnership with one or more mission agencies. As one veteran mission leader comments, "If governments ran wars the way some churches do missions, they would just hand out rifles and airplane tickets to soldiers and expect them to go win the war with little training, no officers, no plans, no organization, and little logistical support."[6]

On the other hand, working with a parachurch organization in no way eliminates the scriptural mandate of being sent out by, and being accountable to, a local church.[7] Some agencies have been careless about honoring their relationship with the church. No matter which sending agency you go with, be sure to maintain a vital relationship with your home church. The agency will supply the needed field training and supervision, but it can never replace the oversight, pastoral care, and encouragement you'll receive from your home leaders. I have always found it very comforting to know that there are people whose first concern is *me*—not my work or ministry.

Get started by examining all your options. An excellent way to begin is through ***relationships.*** While you should not automatically join an organization simply because you have friends in it, relationships are a surprisingly healthy way to choose a team or organization. If you are drawn to people you've met because of common vision and values, there's a good chance the organization will also hold many of those same values. Also, a healthy relationship, whether one of respect for a seasoned worker or a peer friendship, will go a long way to ensure success during your first term, assuming you will be working with that individual.

---

6   Rick Brown, personal correspondence.

7   Johnstone gives some excellent guidelines for the kind of accountability churches should require of mission agencies. The agencies must have the attitude of serving, rather than by-passing, the local church. *The Church is Bigger than You Think*, chapter 19.

If you have absolutely no idea where to begin, don't panic! There are some excellent resources available to get you started. *Operation World* has a list and contact information for dozens of mission organizations.[8] One of many useful websites is www.missionaryresources.org.[9] Depending on where you live, there may be regional organizations that partner with all the local agencies. For example, two well-known organizations in Latin America are COMIBAM and FEDEMEC, whose goals are to recruit and train Hispanic cross-cultural missionaries.

Another suggestion is to attend a missions conference. (The most well known in the United States is the Urbana Student Missions Convention, held in Urbana, Illinois, each December.) Usually various agencies will set up displays that offer information about their ministry, with material you can take home to study. Take every opportunity to speak with individual missionaries, whether at a conference or after a church service. Ask if you can correspond by e-mail. They will usually be delighted to talk about their work. Learn where they live, what they're doing, and why they chose their parent organization. The more people you meet from a given organization, the better idea you'll have of their "flavor".

Narrowing the field. Now we'll look at some practical ways that you can focus in on some organizations and eliminate some others. But before beginning, let's remember the most important principle—prayerfully seeking God for ***His*** direction. He will be faithful to lead you to the right people and to speak to your heart. He may, in His sovereign wisdom, "override" some of the guidelines listed below. That's fine! You'll know that God has a purpose in His choice. In general, though, there are some factors that you'll want to consider.

---

8 *OperationWorld*, Appendix 3.

9 This website not only lists a number of mission agencies, but has a wide range of practical information and resources for future and current missionaries.

a) **Nature and location of the organization's work.** This is the simplest and most obvious way to narrow the field. If your burden is for Thailand, you won't choose Arab World Ministries. If you want to do Bible translation, a medical mission is probably not for you. Although hopefully all mission organizations will have the shared goal of seeing the spread of God's kingdom the growth of His church, many participate in this global task in a specialized role. Some agencies focus on church planting, others on relief work, development, or education. Some work only in certain geographical areas. Examine your own vision, and decide what you're seeking. Do you want to participate in a certain type of ministry Do you hope to utilize your professional skills? Are you called to a particular geographical location, world religion, or ethnic group? Do you want to work with a specific socioeconomic level (the poor vs. professionals, rural vs. urban, etc.)? Compare each agency's specific vision with your own.

b) **Doctrine.** Please don't take any short cuts on this one! An acquaintance of mine had made plans to join a particular mission organization. He was thrilled that he would be able to use his professional skills in a restricted access nation. Although he was from a charismatic background and the organization was not, he felt that that would not be an issue. He quit his job and began the process of packing and saying goodbye. Just days before his scheduled departure, he received his personnel packet, including a doctrinal statement to be signed. To his great dismay, he was asked to agree that he would not use a particular spiritual gift, even in private. His conscience would not allow him to sign the statement, and that was the end of that! Later, he did go on to become a successful missionary with another group, but it was a painful and costly episode.

I know those long doctrinal statements can be dry, but read through them carefully. Every agency should have one, and you should be able to access it on their website. If not, contact them and request one. First, be sure that the organization holds to the basic foundations of Biblical

Christianity. Then check for their position on some of the issues that might be more controversial. Some questions have been debated by sincere Christians for centuries and are not likely to be settled soon. Other areas seem to pop up as current "hot" issues. As I'm writing, a few of these today are: models for child rearing, the role of women in ministry, issues of divorce and re-marriage, church planting methods, degrees of contextualization, and the list goes on!

Whatever your personal convictions, do not bring division to the field. You are going as a servant, not as a reformer, so if there's something you absolutely can't agree on, find another organization! The majority of parachurch agencies are inter-denominational and require agreement on the basic tenets of the Christian faith. Others, however, are more sectarian in their doctrinal positions. Those who plan to be directly involved in church planting will particularly want to consider doctrinal points as they decide whether they can embrace the pattern of church to be established.

c) Values and lifestyle. Beyond doctrine, most agencies or churches have a set of values and methods that determine how they live and carry out their ministry. Some organizations will have written statements of values; *all* will have an intangible, unspoken "style". Learn all you can from the agency's website, but then try to spend some time with some of their workers. How do they relate to one another? Are they on a first-name basis, or more formal? Is there genuine friendship among them, or are they merely colleagues? What is the balance between enjoying a sense of humor and being serious-minded? How do they feel about youth? Older people? Women? Are they open to radical new ideas, or are they more conservative? Are they tough-minded pioneers or more group-oriented? What is their lifestyle on the field? Are they living together in compounds or scattered in the community? Are their living conditions similar to Western standards or more basic? And so on. Find an organizational culture that you will be comfortable with.

d) Gender and family roles. Some organizations expect the wife to work full-time in the ministry, even if there are small children. At the other end of the scale are agencies that do not endorse the wife's participation outside of the home. For all women, both single and married, there is much debate about women's roles, particularly in leadership, preaching, and teaching. Be sure that you are comfortable with an agency's stance in these areas. Finally, investigate the options (and support) available for your children's care and education.

e) Prerequisites. What are the agency's entry requirements? Do they require a college degree or professional experience? Seminary courses? Field training? Is language school required? What is the time commitment for the first term on the field? Do they have opportunities for short-term service? Do they have a minimum (or maximum) age? What is the application process? If this is your first assignment and you're still in the exploration phase, you may want to try a shorter term commitment initially, and then go back for further training. (We'll explore the training issue in depth in chapter 6.)

By now you're getting the picture that you should take time to learn all you can about an organization! This is especially important if you are looking to make a long-term commitment. **Other factors you should check out are:**

- How large is the organization?

- When, how and why were they founded?

- Are they growing? How and where?

- What percentage of workers leaves the organization each year, and why (retirement, job dissatisfaction, health problems, etc.)?

- What is their organizational structure and leadership style?

- Are the teams multi-national or primarily Western, Latino, Asian, etc.?

- What kind of field support and pastoral care are provided?
- Are their members salaried or volunteers? Is a minimum budget required?

As you process all the information that you gather, remember that GOD is the ultimate decision maker! He may lead you into what appears to be an imperfect match to bring about growth and change in your life. Prayerfully submit your search process, as well as your decisions, to the Lord of the harvest.

STEP 7

CHOOSE A TEAM

You will probably have to repeat most of the research process as you move from your organizational choice to your selection of a field team. Even within an organization, there can be wide variations among teams in ministry styles, lifestyles, and team dynamics. If at all possible, meet the team members on their "turf," even if that means making a rather expensive trip. How do they interact? Are there frictions? What is their lifestyle? What kinds of churches are they working with or seeking to plant? What methods are they using? And so on. In other words, carefully repeat each of the questions discussed in step 6.

In addition to the questions already listed, *take time to get to know the team leader.* Can you trust his (or her) integrity? What about his leadership style? Is it authoritative or participatory? Does he have administrative gifts? A pastoral heart? Does he facilitate growth in ministry? How do the other team members feel about him? I have had the joy of serving under gifted and loving men and women, and flourishing under their leadership. But I have also suffered the personal devastation of working under immature and abusive leaders, and would certainly not choose the experience for a new recruit. Do all that you can to determine the overall spiritual and relational health of a team before signing on.

STEP 8

BEGIN THE APPLICATION PROCESS

Now you're ready to begin the application process. Since you have already researched the organizations you are interested in, you are probably familiar with each agency's particular requirements. ***Of course the selection process is a two-way street.*** As you are "checking out" the organization, they'll want to learn about *you*. A good agency will want to know about your beliefs, background, experience and education, and will certainly want to check references from your pastor and others. The application process may include a series of interviews, psychological testing, or an on-site visit to the field. It will be helpful for you to find out ahead of time precisely what will be expected during the application procedure so that you can be prepared.

Although you may feel uncomfortable with some aspects of the process, bear in mind that the agency's cautiousness is for both your protection and theirs. You *should* be concerned if there is little or no checking on "who you are". This may be an indication of carelessness about administration, or worse, about people. As in all that you do on your road to missions, work prayerfully and involve your family, leaders, and godly friends.

Don't forget to enjoy the journey. Your search for an agency and the application process need not be tedious. As you conduct your research, you'll get to learn about what God is doing in and through a wide variety of groups, and to meet some fascinating people. I had this experience following my internship in North Africa. I interviewed with several teams to find the right one for me. Along the way, I rejoiced in just how many flavors were at work in a single city, each one reaching a different stratum of society. I was privileged to meet some incredibly dedicated Christians, whose sacrificial lifestyle made a deep and lasting impression on me. And having learned about the various projects and groups, I am better able to pray for their work.

BEFORE MOVING ON...

Have you and your pastor discussed the type of organization you will work with?

Have you looked into various options available to you?

As you narrow your search, have you carefully studied the doctrinal position and philosophy of the organizations that you are considering?

Have you researched the other points listed in this chapter?

Have you corresponded with the team that you are thinking of working with? (If at all possible, visit!)

Have you determined that the team is healthy?

Have you found out what the application procedure is for the agency you have chosen?

MAPPING THE ROAD TO SUCCESS

CHAPTER SIX

I anxiously scanned the crowd at the international airport, looking for Flor.[1] I was really excited about her arrival. Flor was a sharp young woman whom I had met the summer before when she had come with a short-term team. God had so touched her heart, that she had returned to her home country, sold her belongings, and taken a YWAM discipleship school. I had invited her back to help coordinate our summer program, followed by a two-month internship in Africa. *There she was! But my delight gradually turned to confusion as I saw her baggage cart with half a dozen large suitcases, and a few carry-ons.* We thought that our communication had been clear about the internship's time-frame, but she explained that she knew she was called to work among the desert people, and had come to stay long-term. She was the first overseas missionary from her church, and they had given her a big send-off party.

Flor successfully completed the summer project and her field practicum; however, the leaders there recommended that she return to her home country to receive additional specialized training, as well as to raise more financial support. Her homecoming at the completion of the five months should have been a joyful celebration of work well done. Regrettably, it turned into an embarrassing and humiliating experience.

---

1   All names in this chapter have been changed, and circumstances have been altered slightly to protect the individuals.

José and Martina's story involved a far more painful outcome. Martina was already an experienced cross-cultural missionary when she met José while ministering in his country. Their mutual passion for God brought them together, and as they made their wedding plans, they also made plans to work in a pioneer area where Martina had felt called since her youth. Like Flor, their intention was to live among the people for many years. José was the first missionary to be sent out by his church, and one of just a few from his nation, so they were sent off with great fanfare and excitement.

Unfortunately, they met with more than their share of troubles: They experienced some difficult illnesses and an unexpected pregnancy. The team leadership was harsh and immature. In addition, the usual culture and language shock were augmented for José because he was the only team member not from Martina's home country. The pressure was overwhelming, yet they felt they had no way out, since they had made a long-term commitment and expectations at home were high. In the end, with José struggling with depression and their marriage near the breaking point, they were forced to leave the field.

Sadly, these stories are not uncommon. Melissa and Bob, a young, newlywed American couple, had a similar experience as they were placed in leadership over a team in Latin America, despite their young age and lack of experience. They, too, had left their home and careers for a lifelong vocation in their new locale. Bob, like José, was overwhelmed by the new culture, and experienced a psychological and spiritual breakdown. The common thread in each of these cases was an overly optimistic long-term plan. *These tragic endings can often be avoided through appropriate short and mid-term goal setting and building.*

The traditional missionary training model usually involves a significant upfront investment in time and money. It generally looks something like this:

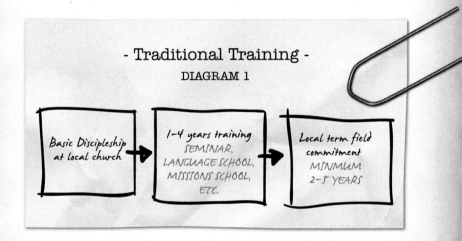

- Traditional Training -

DIAGRAM 1

| Basic Discipleship at local church | 1-4 years training SEMINAR, LANGUAGE SCHOOL, MISSIONS SCHOOL, ETC. | Local term field commitment MINIMUM 2-5 YEARS |

The long training time in this model can place heavy demands on the new missionaries to succeed and "pay back" through their time on the field. If for whatever reason they are struggling in their assignment, they are often reluctant to return home, knowing that they will battle a sense of disappointment and failure, both internal and external. So, like Martina and José or Melissa and Bob, they stay longer than is wise and risk a total breakdown.

A healthier model involves a core of basic discipleship at home, and then a cycle of increasing time periods on the field alternating with more structured training, as shown in Diagram 2.

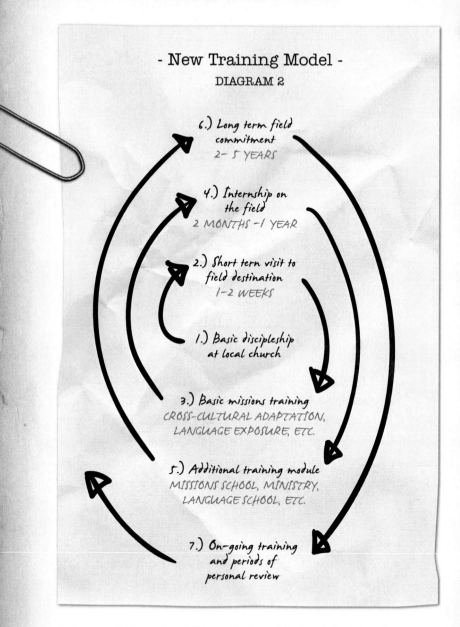

- New Training Model -
DIAGRAM 2

6.) Long term field
commitment
2 – 5 YEARS

4.) Internship on
the field
2 MONTHS – 1 YEAR

2.) Short term visit to
field destination
1 – 2 WEEKS

1.) Basic discipleship
at local church

3.) Basic missions training
CROSS-CULTURAL ADAPTATION,
LANGUAGE EXPOSURE, ETC.

5.) Additional training module
MISSIONS SCHOOL, MINISTRY,
LANGUAGE SCHOOL, ETC.

7.) On-going training
and periods of
personal review

What are the benefits of this cyclical model of training? One important advantage of initial shorter-term commitments is related to expec-

tations. In fact, failed expectations are a significant factor in newer missionaries leaving the field, particularly those from new sending countries.[2] No matter how much you study ahead of time, you can only surmise about life on the field, and your ideas will often be colored by zeal and excitement. It is simply impossible to *really* know just how you will fit into a team, project, culture or country until you have lived there. Even a visit will probably not take you past the "honeymoon" phase to "real life". Your own expectations may also be compounded by the idealism of your supporters and sending church. That's why I recommend planning for an initial commitment of two months to a year—that way, you'll be able to realistically assess the situation (as well as your personal gifts, shortcomings, and calling). If circumstances aren't as you had thought or hoped, you will have the option of a gracious and healthy exit, having successfully completed your first term. You can then make yourself available to God for another assignment or further preparation.

Second, we learn best by practicing and doing. Most of us can only remember a fraction of what we are taught in a classroom. The traditional model of missionary training is theory-heavy. The student is inundated with theoretical instruction, with little or no opportunity to put it into pr actice. Take some basic classes, apply what you learn overseas, and then return for more specialized training. Think of it as building a strong wall. Each training module is like a concrete block; hands-on experience is like the cement that makes it stick together. Continue to train, work, and come back for more advanced learning. Once you are on the field and involved in ministry, you also will have a better understanding of what kind of additional instruction will be most useful to you.

---

2   Taylor, p. 222-223, 244.

Many mission agencies are switching to the newer training model, some by choice, others out of necessity: **today's young people are opting for initial trial periods, time-specific projects, and, in general, shorter terms on the field.**[3] Some older missionaries are quick to judge this trend as a lack of dedication on the part of the youth; but on the flip side is their legitimate concern to gather information before making a lengthy commitment, as well as a desire to see their service count in concrete, measurable ways. Whatever the reasons, this trend is today's reality, and church and missions leaders need to seek creative ways to recruit, equip, and retain young workers.

Are you ready to get started on your **planning?** Not all of you will choose to follow the model I've presented; your church or agency may not offer that option; but I hope you will consider the principles involved. Work together with your church leaders and your sending agency to carefully map out your pathway to long-term missions. Develop a tentative plan that includes both theoretical and field experience, with debriefing and re-evaluation built in after each phase.

STEP 9

ASSESS YOUR TRAINING NEEDS

Let's begin with the kind of formal preparation you'll probably want to get in your home country. In step 10, we'll go on to discuss getting on-the-field experience and coaching.) Some questions to ask yourself are:

a) How much preparation do I need, and when? The answer will be a highly individualized one, depending on the type of ministry you plan to enter, previous experience or instruction, gaps in your

---

3   See Kath Donovan and Ruth Myors' excellent analysis of generational trends in missions. "Reflections on Attrition in Career Missionaries: A Generational Perspective Into the Future", Taylor, p. 41f.

overall preparation, and of course, the prerequisites of your church or mission agency. Ideally, you should achieve proficiency at home for whatever you'll be doing on the field, before having to accomplish it cross-culturally and in another language. This is true of both ministry activities and professional or tent-making skills.

The danger in the area of training usually lies in either of the two extremes: On the one hand, some workers arrive on the field with no ministry or professional background or they are completely unprepared for cross-cultural, social, and language adaptation. On the other hand, others spend years in preparation, whether in language study or in seminary, only to realize after a few short months on the field that this isn't what they are called to do.

b) **What kind of training do I need, and where can I get it?** There are several areas that you will want to consider. As you review the list of recommended training below, don't be alarmed—you don't need to become an expert in everything all at once, but you do want to fill in any glaring holes. Be sure to discuss each of the training components with your church leadership, and find out what your mission agency, denomination, or team requires or recommends.[4] What is essential to get started? What additional courses will you want to take down the road? Some components may be available right at home. Some may be offered by your denomination or mission agency. You may choose to put together a patchwork of modules, taking advantage of a variety of seminars, programs, and resources.

---

4   Hoke and Taylor include an excellent appendix showing the training paths suggested by a number of the larger mission agencies. In addition, they present a comprehensive list of the character qualities, ministry skills, and knowledge components expected of successful candidates (p. 26-27). Ferris shares similar candidate profiles from organizations in Argentina and India (p. 147-159).

Recommended training components:

- **Personal character and interpersonal relation-ships.** I've put this top on the list because it is absolutely essential for fruitfulness and longevity on the field, yet it is rarely included in mission training programs.[5] Hopefully, you have received some good personal discipleship at your local church, but if you still have any serious emotional problems or difficulty in relating to others, be sure to get help *before* heading to the field.

- **Bible Doctrine and Theology.** Every Christian needs to build a solid Biblical foundation, and also an understanding of the nature of the church. But you *don't* need a PhD in theology to be a missionary, particularly if you will be involved in a support role, such as hospitality, computer technician, accountant, etc. Many churches offer excellent Bible teaching, and this may be all you need. Those going into fields such as church planting, Bible translation, or leadership development may wish to consider more formal courses provided through a Bible college, seminary, or correspondence course.

- **Cross-cultural adaptation.** The ability to interpret—and adapt to—cultural differences is an extremely valuable tool for every overseas worker. Most mission training programs will include a module on this important topic. You can begin building your cultural skills informally right at home by developing friendships across racial, economic, linguistic, or cultural barriers in your home town and taking notes on cultural differences. Taking short term trips to other countries is another excellent beginning.

---

5   There are some exceptions. For example, YWAM's Discipleship Training School has a strong emphasis on relationships, personal disciplines, and character building..

- Knowledge of the specific culture you'll be entering. You can begin at home by reading about the people group you'll be working with, including their customs, religion, government, etc. Your team may be able to provide you with study resources or request that you attend workshops or seminars. This kind of instruction will go a long way toward easing your culture shock, preventing cultural bloopers, and making your presentation of the Gospel more effective

- Language learning. Many organizations require intensive language study (six months to two years) *before* beginning your ministry assignment, whether at a language school, or through a dedicated time on the field. Upfront language study will naturally make your adjustment quicker and easier. However, unless you're 100% sure of your long range goals, it's better to start with a basic exposure to the language; then, test your calling through an internship period, and afterwards continue with more formal language study. Many missions training programs will also include a helpful module on *how* to learn a language.

- Specialization related to your ministry area. Depending on the focus of your team, you may want training in church planting methods, primary health care, counseling, linguistics, educational principles, leadership development, etc.

- Professional and technical training. Do you have a valuable skill to bring to your team? In particular, groups working in restricted-access nations often need to offer a tangible benefit to the people. Generations ago, this was generally limited to medicine and education. However, nowadays anything from managing a restaurant to computer skills to an aptitude in sports can open a door. In today's global economy,

English teachers are welcomed just about anywhere in the world.[6] Find out what the needs are where you want to work; then take stock of your abilities, gifts, and interests—when do you "shine" most? Once you've got a goal, pursue the necessary training, but be careful not to get way-laid on a career track!

In summary, take one chunk of training at a time and avoid getting side-tracked from your vision by *too much* preparation. Let's go on to discuss why and how to get practical on-the-field training and coaching.

STEP 10

ARRANGE FOR AN ON-FIELD INTERNSHIP

Most people are familiar with short-term mission trips (one to three weeks in length). These are an excellent introduction to the challenges (and delights!) of sharing the Gospel cross-culturally. Before you make a final decision concerning a longer-term commitment to a team or location, *I strongly encourage you to make at least one short-term visit to your potential destination.* This will help you get a clearer understanding of the physical and spiritual aspects of the area, and at least some concept of what it would be like to live there. It will also enable you to get to know the team and leadership, and answer some of the questions listed in chapters 5 and 9.

However, even several short-term visits are unlikely to get you past the "honeymoon" phase. *Neither formal training nor short visits can fully prepare you for the barrage of cultural and spiritual demands you will face in your new setting.* "Survival" and personal adaptation

---

6   As an experienced ESL (English as a Second Language) teacher, I would encourage new workers to look at some of the excellent short-term training opportunities available. Only in rare cases is a Master's degree required to teach overseas.

are only the beginning. You will need to learn to effectively present the Gospel, verbally and as a living witness, in a world that will initially seem bizarre and confusing. Effective strategies may vary for different economic classes, castes, and tribes; for secular or religious individuals; for people of different age groups; etc., etc.! Those who have arrived ahead of you have probably spent considerable effort to understand these issues, and undoubtedly have learned from numerous mistakes. They will want to help you avoid the same pitfalls and help you become productive as quickly as possible.

The best way to become a serious student of the culture as well as to learn the ropes of the ministry is through a period of internship. In an internship, sometimes referred to as being mentored, the trainee first *observes* the mentor at work. Soon he is able to *help* the mentor. Next the mentor gives the intern an assignment and helps him to complete it. Finally, the trainee is able to *carry out the work himself,* with the mentor giving constructive feedback.

Being mentored also helps us to learn ministry principles and develop godly character traits. There are numerous Biblical examples of mentoring: Joshua learned from Moses; Elisha and a whole group of prophets lived and worked with Elijah; Timothy and others went on the road with Paul. Of course, Jesus is our model of the perfect coach. He instructed and modeled ministry to His disciples; later He sent them out on a field assignment and debriefed them on their return; and finally, He commissioned them to work on their own. All of us should be willing to become learners, particularly as we shift to a new ministry.

A healthy field apprenticeship is generally marked by two characteristics:

- The new worker assumes the attitude and position of a learner and profits from the opportunity to work alongside, and learn from, experienced workers. Yes, you will be serving, but your primary focus is learning from others!

- **The apprenticeship is limited to a specific time period**, preferably two to six months, a year at the most—long enough to learn about "real life", but short enough to have a definite ending and gracious exit before a re-evaluation of long-term possibilities.

Why are internships so uncommon? Many churches and organizations are sending new teams directly into frontier areas, skipping the apprenticeship phase. Perhaps it is due to their rightful zeal to fulfill the Great Commission and to speedily get teams out to the unreached. Perhaps it is because the nature of pioneer missions requires a go-anywhere, do-anything, rough, tough attitude. But we need to be careful to generously lace these attitudes with ***humility***.[7] We North Americans have the worst reputation for arrogance, but pride crosses international borders.

Ignoring the wisdom of more experienced workers will lessen your team's fruitfulness, and may come with a high price tag. A lack of understanding of the day-to-day realities of the region will almost always result in missionary casualties—not only workers leaving the field prematurely, but also leaving messes for other workers to clean up. I was witness to one such breakdown ...

---

[7] I want to commend the Radicals Project (under the auspices of World Horizons) in Brazil. They have designed a thorough and rigorous training program that includes an extensive internship with existing teams in frontier situations. At the time that they initiated their program, most of these teams were led by Westerners, so the students were required to learn English or French before commencing their apprenticeship. Praise God that the number of Brazilian (and other Latin) teams in frontier missions is multiplying exponentially. This intermediate step may soon be irrelevant, but I appreciate the humility of the Radicals Project's leaders and their openness to learn from more established mission organizations. We have a lot to learn from them!

This team of zealous young people was ready to go. "Frontier missions" was their buzzword; their attitude was, "We can do it!"[8] Even though there were several highly experienced teams in the city where they were headed, they chose to establish themselves independently, even bypassing their own organization's structure. They immediately stirred up controversy by living in a co-ed housing situation, unaware that it was taboo in the culture. Soon, one of the young women was devastated by an incident of sexual harassment. She didn't know that a woman should never let a strange man through the door. Their naïveté about the society's corruption caused their humanitarian project to lose thousands of dollars. Several of the team went home early due to discouragement. At the end of their two-year commitment, only a couple of team members chose to stay on. The other mission teams in the city were left to deal with the negative testimony created in the community.

Are there legitimate reasons for not starting out alongside an experienced ministry? The team may have a mandate to initiate a new project or ministry. Or in a true frontier situation, there may be no existing teams in the target area. However, there is usually a team within the region that is working with a closely related people group or project that would be willing to apprentice new workers. In other cases, the sending organization wants to send *an entire team*, making an internship more challenging. It may take some research, but if you're willing to search, there **are** teams out there that are ready and willing to coach an entire group and later joyfully release them to establish their own ministry.[9]

---

8   Circumstances are altered slightly to maintain anonymity.

9   I had the privilege of participating in a successful training model through YWAM with a group of Latin Americans headed into a true pioneering situation—we knew of no established teams within their target area. After completing their theoretical instruction and short-term outreach, they joined me in a neighboring country for intensive coaching in cultural adaptation and exposure to the target language. After two and a half months, they successfully initiated their own project

Wrapping up: some practical pointers. Just how should you go about organizing your internship? You'll want to *find a mature and welcoming leader* or experienced worker who has the time and inclination to receive, coach and train you. Ideally, the team you hope to join on a long-term basis will be willing to help. If, however, due to a heavy workload or other pressures, they are unable to make this commitment, ask them to help you locate another team working within the same or similar culture. The parent organization, your church, or your denomination may also be able to match you with some seasoned workers. A number of mission agencies offer short-term service assignments with this kind of exposure in mind.[10] Before making your decision, clearly communicate with those on the receiving end. Let them know your hopes and desires, and find out what they will be expecting of you. *And of course, pray, asking God to provide just the right field experience!*

---

across the border. World Horizons is another organization willing to intern entire teams; I'm sure there are others.

10   Including Wycliffe, Christian Missionary Alliance, Assemblies of God, New Tribes Missions, YWAM, World Horizons, and I'm sure many others.

BEFORE MOVING ON...

Have you and your church leaders assessed
your training needs?

Have you researched the training requirements of
your mission agency, denomination, or team?

Have you decided which training components
you should take up front and which you should
take later?

Have you looked into where you can get the training
you want, and started the application process?

Have you begun looking for a suitable
internship opportunity?

WHO'S HOLDING THE ROPES?

CHAPTER SEVEN

Gathered in a small circle, the ladies prayed for the church's missionaries, as they did every Tuesday. This particular evening they sensed God leading them to pray for Rick and Lenore, a couple working in a remote village in the Sahel region of Africa. As they interceded, one woman had a picture of a huge black snake. Thinking it symbolic for the work of the enemy, the group asked God for protection and safety for the family. Curious, the group later wrote inquiring if anything in particular had happened on that date. In those days, mail could take many weeks, but when the return mail finally arrived, they were astounded to discover that at about the same time as the prayer meeting, Rick had found a large, black venomous snake in their garden, just feet away from their young daughter!

Whether your next step is formal training, an internship, or a longer-term assignment on the field, strong support from the home front is an essential component of a successful ministry plan. Anyone who has watched an emergency rescue knows that it's a team effort. If you are assigned to recover an injured hiker at the bottom of a cliff, you want to know that your safety ropes are secure, that your squad is on alert at the top, and that everyone is trained in their role, ready to pull you back up in case of an unforeseen crisis. *Missions, like rescue operations, involves venturing into dangerous areas to save lives.* While your assignment may not have a high risk of physical danger (although many assignments do), you *will be* entering enemy territory. Having a team at home base committed to holding your ropes is indispensable. Independence is not an option!

I am guessing that, having worked this far in the book, you're probably itching to get off and running, but don't neglect this crucial phase of preparation. *For a "full-powered" mission, you'll want to enlist partners for at least four areas of home support: prayer backing, finances, pastoral care, and practical help.*

STEP 11
———

BUILD A SECURE PRAYER NETWORK

Most mission organizations require new workers to raise adequate financial support before heading to the field (which, by the way, is usually a healthy practice which we'll address in chapter 9). But, sadly, few organizations have any stipulations about developing adequate prayer support. I was surprised, therefore, when I applied to attend a YWAM School of Frontier Missions and we were required to develop a group of intercessors **before** coming to the school. While finances and other support roles are important, having a strong backing of intercession is absolutely vital to your success on the field. *Prayer—yours and others'—should be the backbone of all that you do.*

The Apostle Paul understood this need. He regularly requested—and thanked the churches for—their prayers:

- For open doors to preach. (Col. 4:3-4)

- For boldness and wisdom in preaching. (Eph. 6:19-20)

- For his safety and service. (Rom. 15:30-31)

- For his deliverance from death. (2 Cor. 1:10-11)

Paul understood that he was involved in a fierce spiritual battle[1] and that an army was required, not a lone solider. He enlisted prayer wherever he went. You, like Paul, will likely be under constant pressure from the enemy, and therefore should have a strong and secure personal intercessory network—individuals and groups committed to pray regularly for you, your family, your colleagues, and your ministry.

Prayer support doesn't just happen. It takes work to develop prayer backing. You'll need to take some practical steps *before* leaving for the field, as well as afterward to maintain communication. Before you begin "recruiting your troops", you'll want to *be prepared to share with folks about your ministry.* Gather and organize your information:

- Who you are (a brief background)
- When and where you're going, and why
- Your ministry focus (the people group you'll be working with,[2] what you'll be doing, etc.)
- Some on-going prayer points

Next, *think creatively about how to present your project.* For group presentations, consider a power-point presentation or video clip so people can visualize your new living situation and the people you'll be ministering to. Another idea is a cultural evening, with the music, food, and apparel of your adopted nationality. Whether you'll be talking to groups or individuals, be sure to produce an attractive prayer card, bookmark, or "refrigerator picture" to leave behind.[3] Let's be honest— even folks who love to pray need a visible reminder from time to time,

---

1   Eph. 6:10-20.

2   Information and prayer profiles are available through the Adopt-a-People-Group Clearinghouse (http://www.adoptapeople.com) and the Joshua Project (http://www.joshuaproject.net).

3   Some excellent ideas and examples are found in the appendices of *Friend Raising*. Barnett, p. 190-191.

and all of us are helped when we are given specific ideas of *how* to pray. If you're like me—neither artistically or technically talented!—find a creative friend to help.

Now you are ready to begin one of the most enjoyable tasks of getting ready to leave: enlisting prayer partners. People who love you will of course want to be involved. But you will be surprised at how many others are excited that they can have a part in what God is doing among the nations. Start by asking *God* to help connect you with people. Then get out your notebook (or your Blackberry if you're not old-fashioned like me) so you can keep track of your contacts. Here are some suggestions for finding partners:

- Begin with the people closest to you. Share your plans and needs and ask if they will commit to pray for you on a regular basis.

- Are there individuals you know who simply love to pray? Retirees in particular find prayer a special way to stay involved in God's work. Even if you don't know the person well, he or she may be delighted to add you to their prayer list.

- Find out what groups meet regularly to pray in your church (or other churches that you know), especially those which focus on missions. Contact the group leaders and ask if their group would be willing to pray for you in their meetings.

- Ask your pastor if you can share with the home groups or other small groups (men's and women's Bible studies, Sunday school classes, college group, children's church, etc.). Some will probably be happy to "adopt" you.

- If your church has a prayer chain, ask permission to send in your prayer requests.

- If your denomination has a mission board, find out if there is an already established prayer network that you can use.

- If you are going to be working among an unreached people group, contact the Adopt-a-People-Group Clearinghouse and ask them to put you in touch with churches or individuals that have adopted your group.

As you develop your list of partners, ask them how often they would be willing to pray for you, the best way to stay in touch, and how to communicate when emergency prayer needs arise. For groups, find out when and how often they meet. Some people may commit to pray monthly, or perhaps when they receive urgent prayer requests. Others may pledge to pray weekly or even daily. Never pressure people for more than they are comfortable with; rather thank them for their participation at whatever level. And, then of course, communicate! (We'll talk more about on-going communication in the next chapter.)

STEP 12
_____

BUILD YOUR FINANCIAL SUPPORT

If you're just starting out, raising your necessary finances can be a daunting task. Westerners may be reluctant to lose their independence; missionaries from nations with struggling economies may not be able to imagine how God can supply; and almost all of us hate the idea of asking for money. *But before we talk about how to raise support, let's talk about* why.

Let's face it—we're human! Just like everyone else, we need to eat, sleep, wear clothes, educate our children, and receive medical attention when ill. In addition, we have many additional expenses related to effectively carrying out our work (travel, language classes, ministry materials, communication, conferences, and so on). And finally, to maintain our spiritual, emotional, and physical health, we need periodic time out for refreshing.

Sadly, ***lack of support is a major reason for missionaries returning home***, particularly those from the newer sending countries in Latin America, Africa, and Asia.[4] Some workers manage to remain on the field, but barely scraping by; their lack of finances takes a toll on their productivity and general well-being. Still others end up being a drain on their teammates when they are unable to meet necessary expenses. Our God is a wonderful, providing God! He does not want to see His children—much less His servants—surviving on breadcrumbs. ***If you are going to carry out the work of the Kingdom, you will need a source of income.***

Some missionaries receive a monthly salary from their denomination or sending organization. Others choose to serve by utilizing their personal savings, the proceeds from the sale of a home, or other outside income, thus freeing up mission funding for other individuals or projects. In recent years, more and more missionaries are seeking paid employment in their host country. Paul himself worked for a time as a tent-maker to support himself.[5] "Tent-making" not only provides a source of income, but can also open many doors of relationships, and may also grant access to countries hostile to the Gospel by supplying a needed service to the community.

Nevertheless, the majority of missionaries are still dependent in part, if not entirely, on gifts and donations, and need to remember that giving and receiving are part of God's pattern for Kingdom work. Even after all these years, I find it awkward to ask concerning my needs. However, the Scriptures make it plain that those who work in the harvest are entitled to financial help:

---

4   "Missionary Attrition: The ReMAP Research Report", Peter W. Brierley, in Taylor, p. 94.

5   Acts 18:3; 2 Thess. 3:7-10.

Don't you know that those who work in the temple get their food from the temple, and those who serve at the altar share in what is offered on the altar? In the same way, the Lord has commanded that those who preach the Gospel should receive their living from the Gospel. (1 Cor. 9:13-24)

The worker [whose work is preaching and teaching] is worthy of his wages. (1 Tim. 5:17-18)

As you step out to develop your financial network, the first and most important principle is to remember that God is your provider. No matter what approach you take, never forget that, ultimately, God is the source. This will help you avoid manipulation, a false reliance on others, and trying to figure things out "your way". The biographies of Hudson Taylor and George Mueller had a tremendous impact on my faith as I prepared for my missions career. These two godly men had learned the secret of utter dependence on God for their needs. In my early years on the field, I had no visible source of income (our church was still maturing in its role of sending), so I *had to* trust in God for my provision. I have treasured memories of the many specific answers to prayers—everything from shoes to airline ticket, as well as things I *didn't* ask for, such as a designated gift to eat out once a month!

As you begin to research the topic of fundraising, I'm sure you will uncover a wealth of practical ideas and methods, but never forget to seek God for guidance in your strategies. Sometimes He will give you explicit instructions about how to approach other people; sometimes He will tell you not to do anything at all, but to wait on Him. But ***He needs to be the One in charge!***

A second key principle is the assurance that it is God's desire for His people at home to be involved in His global task. My brother-in-law gave me a fresh perspective when he reminded me that churches and individuals involved in missions are participating in God's passion, so He will be faithful to reward them, both in their finances and fruitfulness. When you enlist givers, you are opening an avenue of blessing for them! Paul shared this same point with the Philippians:

> *Not that I am looking for a gift, but I am looking for what may be credited to your account... The gifts you sent are a fragrant offering, an acceptable sacrifice, pleasing to God.* **And my God will meet all your needs according to His glorious riches in Christ Jesus.** *(Philip. 4:17-18. Emphasis mine.)*

Like your intercessors, your financial supporters will have a special place in your life and ministry. In her book *Friend Raising*, Betty Barnett emphasizes the importance of personal connection and involvement:

> *Using the term 'friend raising' rather than 'fund raising' captures the essence of support raising... We are called to a lifestyle of exchange—of giving and receiving. The Lord's business is raising our resources; we are to build relationships as He leads. By seeking to serve our friends, we give them opportunities to share in our lives and ministries... .***Many people who have no access to overseas ministry would respond positively to a trustworthy avenue for personal involvement in world missions—if they only knew how."**[6] *(Emphasis mine.)*

So what's the first step? One of the first things you'll want to do (after prayer, of course) is develop a detailed budget. This will help you accurately assess your needs and answer questions that may arise. Some organizations have strict rules requiring you to have a certain percentage of your budget committed ahead of time. This is for your protection, as well as your co-workers'—arriving without sufficient funds can be a strain on everyone. Other agencies are quite lenient. Either way, you should still go prepared. Chapter 9, along with Appendix D, presents

---

6   *Friend-Raising: Building a Missionary Support Team that Lasts*, p. 23-24, 56.

guidelines for the budgeting process. You may want to work on those chapter steps as you continue to work through this chapter.

Once you know how much funding you'll need, meet with your pastor or missions committee. It's important that your home church be involved in giving, even if they can only contribute in a small way initially. This will help the congregation expand their vision and participation outside of their community, and will also reaffirm their connection and commitment to you. And of course, giving will bring a returned blessing! Some congregations choose to provide directly to their missionaries with a monthly stipend or through periodic special offerings. Others encourage their missionaries to solicit from individuals within the church. Find out what your church's policy is, and what role they will have in financing your ministry.[7]

Next, follow the same ideas and guidelines that you did to enlist prayer partners: pray, prepare, and talk with individuals and groups you think will be interested. In fact, you may find that your list of givers overlaps considerably with your list of intercessors. You don't need to limit your network to church members, or even Christians, for that matter. There are numerous books available on raising your needed finances, so I will not elaborate on the wide array of methods and ideas that are suggested. My personal favorite is *Friend Raising*, which I strongly recommend to both new and veteran missionaries. Barnett beautifully interweaves Biblical principles with loads of helpful tips, useful forms, and encouraging testimonies. Get your hands on a copy as soon as you can!

---

7   I personally recommend that the church as an organization contribute at some level. This means *all* of the members are involved, at least indirectly. If your church has never supported a missionary, you may need to gently communicate the benefits of giving and sending. Share this and other books that convey the role of the sending church. One excellent resource is Pirolo's *Serving as Senders.*.

Hopefully, you will find the process of "friend raising" to be a joyful one, and will quickly secure the pledges that you need. However, **what happens if you aren't able to raise enough funds?** Don't let the financial hurdle be your first consideration. I had been on the field for a while when I chose to join YWAM. As a pre-requisite I needed to attend a Crossroads Discipleship Training School. The cost, including airfare, was several thousand dollars. It might as well have been a million! My regular pledges barely covered my day-to-day expenses. Still, I was convinced that the school—and working with YWAM—was part of God's plan for me. As I sought the Lord, He instructed me to ask *Him* for the provision, rather than others. Little by little funds came in, but I was still a thousand dollars short the week before the school. The *day* before my flight I received a check for the exact amount. Later I discovered that a member of a supporting church was awakened in the middle of the night—to pray for my finances! It was her church that made the gift.

If you are below your budget level, there are several alternatives that you will need to prayerfully consider. Maybe God wants you to continue working to secure more pledges, or to press in more deeply in prayer. Perhaps you need to look again at your itemized expenses, and trim any unnecessary costs. God might be using the situation to test your faith—Are you willing to step out and trust Him for the rest to come in later? On the other hand, it could be a sign that "right now" is not His timing, particularly if your agency requires fully committed backing. Be sure to make this decision through prayer and discussion with your family, your field team, and your home leaders.

Throughout your support-raising process, be encouraged that the LORD is your shepherd—He is faithful to lead, to guide, and to provide!

BEFORE MOVING ON...

Have you developed a network of groups and individuals who are committed to pray for you?

Have you read FRIEND RAISING, by Betty Barnett, or a similar guide to building financial partnerships?

Have you shared with your pastor or other church leaders about your proposed budget and financial needs?

Have you raised sufficient financial pledges to begin your journey? If not, have you shared and prayed with your home and field leaders?

Note: You may want to work through the budgeting process in Chapter 9 before completing the last two activities.

WHO'S HOLDING THE ROPES?
(CONTINUED)

CHAPTER EIGHT

Things weren't going as I had hoped. In fact, they weren't going very well at all! I had enrolled in an intensive training program to prepare me for my move to North Africa. The invited lecturers were each outstanding in their fields and I was excited about all I was learning. However, the school leaders were inexperienced, and there were some painful interpersonal conflicts. It was a confusing and difficult time for me, and I began to lose my confidence of who I was in Christ. In a word, I was floundering. I knew I needed help from home.

It seems laughable now, but the only way for me to make a private call was to place a collect call from an outside pay phone around the corner. I'll never forget standing out on the street, with my pastor's words resonating across the Atlantic: *"Marcia, I can be there on the next flight if you want me to."* Waves of affirmation washed over me, and I knew I was going to make it. No, I didn't need him to come, but his solid commitment and faith in me were a lifeline. Many more calls were placed from that outside phone to friends, leaders, and prayer partners. The safety rope held firm.

SECURE YOUR LINES OF
ENCOURAGEMENT AND COUNSEL

Simple words of encouragement or an expression of concern can be lifelines in our difficult moments. Are there folks who are committed to stick with you throughout your adventures? People who will cheer you on, but also bring words of correction when necessary? Over the years I've met numerous missionaries from a wide variety of backgrounds, and am aware that many don't have the blessing of a strongly supportive church or pastor. Some have no home church at all; others are receiving nominal or halfhearted backing, or come from such a large church that their pastor barely knows them; and many have gone through the distress of church splits, pastors leaving, and so on.

Even if your situation is less than ideal, be sure to secure commitments from mature men and women of God to be your source of counsel. Hopefully, as you have worked through the earlier chapters in this book, you have been consistently strengthening your relationships with your pastor, leaders, and other godly people. You'll need their encouragement and advice in difficult times. But even more importantly, they will serve as a rope to pull you back in if you begin to "drift". When you are far from home, far from your church family, adapting to a strange and confusing culture, and under pressure from the enemy, it is so easy to gradually slip into small areas of deception, those little "gray" areas of morals and doctrine. It has happened to me; it happens to all of us. Often, we're not even aware that we're drifting into dangerous currents. Timely advice from a trusted individual back home can be the needed tug to pull us back to safety.

Meet with your leaders and let them know that you want to be accountable. Verbally, or even in writing, commit to keep them informed on a regular basis, and *especially* when things aren't going well. It's in the hard times that we are most tempted to "hide out", and then that we most need godly input. Give them permission to ask you tough questions about your spiritual health, your physical health, your family and team life, your ministry. Commit to follow their counsel, even if you may not totally agree. Remember, accountability is your protection from self-deception. Ask them to pledge *their* commitment to pray for you, to check up on you regularly, and to speak into your life when they see any areas of concern. Then work together to keep your connection strong.[1]

By the way, some of my most gratifying experiences have been the times that my leaders and other friends and supporters have come to visit me in various field locations. What a blessing that they cared enough to want to learn about my work and life! They were able to return home with a clearer understanding of how to pray and also how to give me wise counsel. And along the way we had great fun as I introduced them to my favorite places, food, and friends! Make a point of inviting your leaders to organize a trip to your new home.

STEP 14

BUILD A TEAM TO HANDLE PRACTICAL MATTERS

In a secular war, logistical personnel are needed to support the front-line soldiers. During World War II, the ratio was about 15 to one. In more recent conflicts, the ratio is closer to 50 support workers per frontline solider.[2] By now you have begun enlisting a home team of intercessors, financial partners, encouragers. But there is one more

---

1   You may wish to give them *Serving as Senders*, by Neal Pirolo, to better acquaint them with their support role.

2   Pirolo, p. 165.

important group.... ***Last, but certainly not least, are those who will administer your day-to-day matters at home.*** When Paul talks about special gifts, he speaks of those whose gift is serving, those able to help others, those who administer.[3] And what a wonderful gift to the Body they are—certainly to us missionaries! When I am overseas, my faithful friend Karen handles all my banking, bills, and mail. Jessica screens my e-mails. Liz takes care of my house. Becky provided foster care for my cats. A trusted Christian CPA handles my taxes. Others have blessed me by getting things ready for my return by setting up appointments, stocking the refrigerator, and leaving flowers and notes of welcome.

These helpers are an indispensable part of every missionary's team. They ensure the efficient flow of our finances, correspondence, and supplies. They remove some of the bumps from our "re-entries". And they give us peace of mind that everything's okay back home. Consider finding people to assist you with each of the following:

- Handling your deposits (including informing you of each donation you receive).
- Checking your incoming mail and paying bills.
- Distributing your newsletters (particularly if you will be working in a restricted country).
- Circulating any special prayer updates.
- Maintaining your home or car.
- Shopping for and shipping any needed supplies.
- Preparing for your home visits (organizing housing, a vehicle, setting up your agenda and appointments, and so on).
- A contact person for emergency evacuation or other crises.

---

3   Rom. 12:7; 1 Cor. 12:28.

Look for individuals who are trustworthy and reliable, and who can keep private matters confidential. Don't overload any one person with too many areas of responsibility—the joy of serving could easily become an uncomfortable burden. I usually ask my partners to commit for a specific time commitment. If you're just starting out, this will normally be your first term abroad. At the end of the time period, release them to decide if they want to continue or not. This also gives *you* a gracious out if they are not handling things as you wish. Perhaps more than any of your other home team members these are the folks who will be making a real sacrifice of time. Remember to express your gratitude on a regular basis.

STEP 15

DEVELOP AND MAINTAIN A SYSTEM OF ON-GOING COMMUNICATION[4]

Have I convinced you of how important your home team is? I hope so! Whether they give financially, pray, or help and encourage in other ways, they are key participants in the work that God has called you to. As your partners, they'll want to be kept informed of your progress, both personal and ministerial. ***It's important that you communicate regularly and creatively.*** I recall one missionary family that I had been supporting monthly for more than a year. I had not received a single letter from them. I felt that they did not regard me as a valuable part of their ministry, and I considered discontinuing my contributions. The next time I saw them at a conference, I confronted them. As it turns

---

4   When I first read *Friend Raising* years ago, I immediately implemented many of Barnett's suggestions on communication, and have been using them ever since. Fifteen years later, it's difficult for me to know just where her ideas leave off, and mine begin. It was refreshing to read her updated version, which includes many helpful tips on e-mail and the Internet. I freely give her credit for much of this section, and once again point you to her book, in particular, chapter 10 on writing newsletters.

out, they did not have a system to know who their gifts were coming from. They rectified the problem immediately, and our friendship has deepened over the years. Your team *deserves* to hear from you!

Most missionaries use periodic newsletters as a form of staying in touch. This is a good starting point. Your letters should encourage your supporters with accounts of what God is doing, but also include some of your struggles. Include interesting stories of your experiences, but be brief. No one (except perhaps your mother) wants to wade through a four-page letter. Let your readers know specific ways to pray, and in the following letter, share how God answered their prayers. Personalize your letters with a short, hand-written note of greeting.

In the days before e-mail was widely available, I would mark my calendar for the date that my letters would arrive home, and knew that shortly afterwards, interesting things would start happening. Again and again, the needed breakthrough—whether for provision, guidance, or removal of an obstacle to ministry—would come within days of my partners receiving my letter. Now, with high-speed technology, we can expect almost immediate prayer coverage and the resulting release or relief.

Another benefit of writing regularly is that you'll be more to likely to *receive* letters. One missionary reported that 47% of the letters he and his family received came within a week of mailing out his prayer letter.[5] This is no luxury on the field. Pirolo shares,

> It is hard to imagine the importance of communication from home until you have "been there". When a person or family arrives on the field ... real loneliness can set in—a feeling of isolation, of being out of touch with—everything! A new missionary can feel, "They have forgotten me!" "They aren't writing" might be interpreted: "They don't

---

5   Pirolo, p. 132-133.

care! I'm out of their sight—and therefore out of their mind! And I am going out of mine!"[6]

Communication is a two-way street, and few letters from home *could be* a result of *you* not taking the initiative.

How often should you send out updates? I recommend preparing a newsletter at least quarterly. If you send e-letters, make sure you find a way to stay in touch with the folks that don't have e-mail. Send a hard-copy letter to everyone at least once or twice a year. Many people like to have a piece of paper and a picture that they can hold in their hands. You should also set up a means of circulating urgent prayer needs that may arise in between your planned mailings.

You will probably want to be in touch with your core team (those who have pledged to pray or to give on a regular basis, close friends, and so on) more frequently. Take a mini-poll and ask them to tell you honestly how often they want to hear from you. Some people I've committed to pray for seem to have fallen off the globe—I rarely get updates, so it's difficult to pray specifically. Others bog me down with lengthy e-mails several times a week. Though I want to stay in touch with them, I don't want this much detail. A lot will depend on their partnership commitment, your level of friendship, and *their* desire for news.

Newsletters are only a starting point. Be creative! Think of fun and imaginative ways to involve your supporters in your new world: send small gifts, handcrafted items, postcards, photos, local stationery, and so on. Some of my colleagues from the desert designed homemade Christmas cards with pictures of the dunes, using glue and real Saharan sand. I've sent gifts of books and videos on missions that I think would interest and motivate my partners. An interactive website is another way to keep your partners involved. Post news, pictures, prayer requests,

---

6   Ibid., p. 121.

contact information, and FAQ's, and update it regularly.[7] Remember to plan for these and other forms of communication in your budget.

Don't forget your grandmother's wise advice: Send thank you notes! For many of today's young people, this is a foreign concept, but gratitude is a godly principle. Your supporters aren't mind readers, and they need to know that you appreciate what they're doing. In your newsletters, thank them for their part in taking the Gospel to the ends of the earth. It's important to send hand-written thank you notes, as well. Do this in response to one-time donations, to those who have helped in a special way, and periodically to your on-going supporters.

No matter how you choose keep people informed, remember that they're friends, not "entities". Use notes, cards, e-mails, and phone calls to stay in touch and strengthen your friendship. Remind them that you want to hear about *their* lives, too, and ask how you can pray for them. ***When you're home for visits, take time to invest in these precious relationships.*** I like to organize social get-togethers to bless my supporters. They enjoy taste-testing typical foods and drinks from where I've traveled, listening to exotic music, and trying on native garments. I usually have little souvenirs for each of them. It's a great time of fun and fellowship, but also a chance for me to express my thanks and for them to learn more about my world. Of course, nothing replaces one-on-one time; if time and distance permit, try to spend quality time with each of your core team members.

---

7   See Barnett, p. 74-75.

BEFORE MOVING ON...

Have you established an accountability relationship with your leaders or other godly friends?

Have you found trustworthy people to take care of practical matters at home?

Have you talked with your partners about how, and how often, you will stay in touch with them?

Have you set up a database or address book so you can regularly communicate with your supporters?

Have you communicated to your partners the specifics of your plans (including ways to pray for you), and thanked them for their participation in your ministry?

BEFORE PACKING YOUR BAGS

CHAPTER NINE

Zap! In just a split second, the damage was done. "José"[1] had plugged in the team's brand new printer. He could see that the outlets were different, so he used a small plug adaptor; however, he didn't realize that the current was 220V, rather than 120V and a transformer would also be needed. Regrettably, the workers receiving José and his team had never thought to inform them of this detail, and it never crossed the team members' minds to ask. Ruining a printer was an expensive error, but not nearly as costly as some mistakes caused by lack of research: offensive cultural blunders, arriving with insufficient funds, or falling in a trap of the devil though unawareness of the spiritual environment.

Have you ever wondered why God ordered Moses to send in twelve spies before invading Canaan?[2] Hadn't God already promised them victory in taking the land? While the Bible doesn't specifically state the reason, we can imagine that He wanted them to gather information that would help them to develop effective battle strategies and to prepare for their new living situation. It was also supposed to encourage them with the good things in store for them, but as we know, the fear of the people turned this last point sour. Moses obeyed God, and gave the spies a list of research questions:

---

1   Names and circumstances changed in this chapter.

2   Numbers 13.

"See what the land is like and whether the people who live there are strong or weak, few or many. What kind of land do they live in? Is it good or bad? What kind of towns do they live in? Are they unwalled or fortified? How is the soil? Is it fertile or poor? Are there trees on it or not? Do your best to bring back some of the fruit of land." (Num. 13:17-20)

"Spy out the land"—Find out everything you possibly can about your destination. Your research list will be more comprehensive than Moses', but with the same aims. Much of what you need to learn can be gathered right at the local library or on your home computer. Of course, by "spying out the land" on a short-term trip, you can supplement your studies with an eyewitness account.

STEP 16

STUDY THE HISTORICAL, CULTURAL, AND SPIRITUAL DYNAMICS OF YOUR NEW LOCATION

Your battle will not be against people, but against the spiritual powers of darkness.[3] In most frontier regions, Satan has held mastery for centuries. Although we know that God has given us His authority to take the land, we do not want to be casual as we enter enemy territory, or be ignorant of the devil's schemes.[4] Do all you can to prepare for the battle by learning what *kind* of influence he has used, and *how* he has held the people captive. This will help you prepare a more effective presentation of the Gospel, as well as prepare you for the kind negative spiritual onslaught you and your family will be facing.

Studying a nation's (or people group's) history, religion, politics, economy, and culture can give you insight into spiritual strongholds, as well as provide you with helpful points for adapting to the society.

---

3   Eph. 6:12.

4   2 Cor. 2:11.

Prayer guides such as *Operation World* or people group profiles are a good place to start,[5] but dig deeper through your own research and reading, using Internet sites and books.[6] Your mission agency and team can probably provide you with some good resources. The more you know, the better equipped you'll be for what lies ahead. Use the list in *Appendix B* as a guideline for your study.

STEP 17

INQUIRE ABOUT LOGISTICAL MATTERS

Transformers, telephones, tickets, towels, toilet paper, and tea—all can affect our adjustment to our new home. Find out what's available, what you'll have to do without, what you can take, and the best way to get it all there! These are a few of the practical questions you'll want to look into. Here are some others:

- Entry requirements and other legal documents
- The best travel routes and luggage restrictions
- Money matters (currency, exchange rate, banking, accessing cash)
- Communication infrastructures
- Security issues (critical in restricted access countries)
- Clothing (taking into consideration both climate and culture)

---

5 *Operation World* has listings by countries, with detailed background on politics, geography, religion, and so on, as well as accounts of what God is doing and current prayer points. Appendix 2 gives informational websites listed by country.

6 The Adopt-a-People Clearinghouse (http://www.adoptapeople.com) and the Joshua Project (http://www.joshuaproject.net) have prayer profiles of thousands of unreached people groups and links to additional websites. The William Carey Library has a fantastic catalog of mission-related books. You can probably find both biographical accounts and strategies for reaching particular groups; for example, there are books on China and Indonesia, on reaching Muslims, Jews, and so on. Visit their website at www.missionbooks.org.

- Educational options for children and language study for yourself

- Health issues and medical care

- Food and drinking water

- Personal items to bring (and not to bring)

- And, of course, electricity!

I've provided a detailed list of questions in **Appendix C** for you to check off. You may think of some additional questions that pertain to your situation.

A well-organized team will have a thorough orientation packet with most of what you'll want to know. But let's face it—lots of teams **aren't** well organized, particularly in a pioneer situation—they're just getting adapted themselves. So you may have to do some of your own research. Thankfully, the Internet makes finding information relatively easy.[7] Even if your team doesn't have an information sheet prepared, they have lots of experience to share. Ask them for help and to confirm what you have found on your own. A short-term visit before your full-time commitment is extremely helpful for getting a "feel" for what life is really like and how to prepare. Whatever approach you take, make sure to get your answers.

If the team leaders send you guidelines and suggestions, follow them! They have learned from trial and error, and are doing their best to make your entry as smooth as possible. If you choose to ignore their recommendations, you are likely to cause headaches both for you and for them. Sadly, my memories of "Priscilla" will always be associated

---

7   A very useful booklet, that is also available online, is "The Missionary Resources Handbook", published by Emercy. Check their website at www.missionaryresources.org. It includes information and resources on topics from passports to insurance to home schooling. Secular travel guides, such as the *Let's Go* and *Lonely Planet* series can also be helpful.

with her unwillingness to follow directions. Instructing her on the best air route to arrive at our remote location, we cautioned her not to take a particular airline, based on many negative experiences. Priscilla used the airline anyway. When her luggage was lost, team members graciously donated some of their clothing. We also explained that, because of our isolated location, there was absolutely no way to receive cash, so she should bring enough money for at least three months' living expenses. When she arrived with only enough funds for a few weeks, the team was obliged to lend her money. *Make your trip—and your welcome—secure through wise preparations.*

STEP 18

PREPARE A DETAILED BUDGET

What do you mean "budget"? I thought missionaries lived "by faith".
All Christians are called to live by faith,[8] whether we live on income we earn in the workplace, on a fixed stipend, or on gifts that fluctuate from month to month. As we discussed in chapter 7, the need for support is a fact of life. Lack of support adds unnecessary stress, and is a major cause for workers leaving the field early.[9] So, yes, this means more research!

Elsa[10] was on the right track. When she applied to join a team located in Europe, she asked the leaders how much she would need for monthly expenses. Her home church was large and prosperous, so it was not difficult to raise the amount they suggested. Alas, the figure they had given her was woefully inadequate—it barely covered the cost of a modest apartment, let alone other living and ministry expenditures.

---

8   Heb. 11:6.

9   "Missionary Attrition: The ReMAP Research Report", Peter W. Brierley, in Taylor, p. 94.

10   Not her real name.

Elsa's budget was so tight she couldn't even afford to buy toothpaste or shampoo, and had to have friends ship them from home! Though the problem was not really her fault, working out a detailed budget, like the one outlined in Appendix D, could have saved her a lot of distress.

However, before sitting down with your calculator, think about the "big picture" and the kind of lifestyle you want to choose. I've met missionaries who lived in mansions with hired servants, others who made the choice to live among the poorest of the poor, and just about everything in between. What is the philosophy of your organization and team? What is your personal philosophy? Is there a range of options for you to choose from? You (and your family, if you're married) will need to prayerfully evaluate your future lifestyle. As you seek the right balance, here are some practical points to think about:

- The standard of living of the people you're trying to reach (e.g., wealthy leaders, professionals, middle class, slum dwellers, refugees, etc.).

- Economy vs. efficiency (e.g., using public transportation vs. owning a vehicle; hand laundry vs. a washing machine).

- Frugality vs. longevity (e.g., sleepless nights vs. air conditioning; emotional burnout vs. regular retreats).

Our most important consideration must be how the way we live will affect our ability to share the Gospel within the culture where we will be living. Missionary trainer Lianne Roembke highlights the fact that lifestyle has a great impact missionaries' credibility as messengers:

> *One of the most critical areas of adjustment, visible to the new community ... is the area of their use of finances and their lifestyle. Their lifestyle, as reflected in their use of money or material resources ... either greatly contributes or erects a great a barrier to credibility in communicating*

the Gospel. It is a high visibility issue and, as such, has the potential of being a great stumbling block in team life, too.[11]

Roembke also warns of dangerous snares in our *attitudes* about money:

Money and lifestyle, though not synonymous, are almost inseparable. The amount of money one has often determines the lifestyle one leads... Greed, as one of the deadly sins, is defined as desiring more than what one has or having more than what is enough in a context when some have less than enough... A preoccupation with material things is also very detrimental to the credibility of the gospel. What constitutes "preoccupation" is also culturally evaluated.[12]

Both our spending habits *and* our attitudes must be weighed Biblically, measuring ourselves within the new culture rather than how we live at home.

In summary, there is no simple "right" answer, although there are some wrong ones. We are called to be good stewards of God's resources, including our body, so we need to avoid extremes. Some workers, particularly young singles, are able to live in remarkably basic conditions, but you will need to decide if this is a healthy long-term solution for you and your family. I've seen fruitful workers at both ends of the lifestyle scale. However, unnecessary extravagance drains mission funding and may separate you from the people you wish to reach. Be sure to discuss your conclusions with your team leaders, as well as your leaders at home.

Now you're ready to get down to specifics. Complete the two worksheets in *Appendix D*—the first is for one-time expenses related to getting

---

11 *Building Multicultural Teams*, p. 167.

12 Ibid., p. 41-42.

to your destination; the second will help you estimate your on-going monthly expenses. Do your best to gather as accurate information as possible. Once you have calculated a detailed budget, submit it to both field and home leaders for their input. Remember, just because you haven't received all your funds, doesn't mean that you can't go. Review the section in chapter 7 on insufficient support. As a good steward, you will also need to develop a system to keep track of your income and expenses; this will enable you to remain accountable to your leaders and supporters, as well as re-evaluate your budget at the end of your first year or term.

BEFORE MOVING ON...

Have you used Appendix B as a guide to study the history, religion, and culture of your people group, and learned some of the ways Satan has worked there?

Have you carefully researched all the practicalities associated with your travel and relocation, using the checklist in Appendix C?

Have you developed a detailed budget, using the worksheet in Appendix D? Have you submitted it to your leaders?

SAYING "GOODBYE" THE RIGHT WAY

CHAPTER TEN

"Rachel"[1] rushed around furiously. With less than two weeks to go before their flight to Africa, there was so much to do! Household items were sorted into various categories: pack, sell, give away, store, and trash. Then of course the long "to-do" list of last minute errands, phone calls, and people to see. With three small children underfoot, it was hard to make much headway. To top it all off, her husband Lee was working long hours at his office, trying to finish a project—Rachel was feeling pretty angry. *No question about it: stress was the predominant emotion of the hour!*

Yet there were so many other emotions that needed to be processed, not only by Rachel, but by Lee and the children: sorrow at saying farewell to loved ones, excitement about their new mission, anxiety concerning the unknown, sadness at leaving favorite places and things behind, gratitude for the Lord's provision, and so on. Not only were feelings shoved to one side; sadly, friends and family took a back seat, too. Sound familiar? It sure does to me! I confess that I tend to operate in the high-speed mode before any major travel, but I'm beginning to learn to make room for my *real* priorities: important relationships, and my own spiritual, emotional and physical well-being.

---

1   Names and circumstances have been altered.

STEP 19

PLAN AHEAD FOR PROPER FAREWELLS

How can you avoid being overwhelmed with last minute tasks? You probably can't eliminate all of the stress, but there *are* things you can do to minimize it. First, build in plenty of extra margin for what you'll need to accomplish. *Have you ever heard of "Murphy's law"?* (Whatever *can* go wrong probably *will* go wrong.) I have developed *"Marsha's law" for packing and moving:* Carefully calculate the amount of time you think it will take you to complete your packing tasks, including some extra time for any mishaps. Take your final figure and double it, figure on a few unexpected emergencies, and you'll be pretty close! I'm joking, of course, but honestly, getting ready to go always seems to take much longer than we think it will, which only adds to our upheaval, so don't cut corners on scheduling time for packing.

More importantly, plan now to make room in your program for people. Do this *before* your life gets too hectic. *Get your calendar out and block out days or evenings for your true treasure: family and friends.* Schedule quality time with the people you'll be leaving behind. This could be "one-on-one" times, or small get-togethers. For example, before one big trip, I organized an intimate dinner with four close girlfriends. I surprised them with personal gifts symbolizing what I most treasured in each of them. This is as much for your friends as for you. They will want to celebrate and mourn, too. Keep in mind that, while you are looking ahead to something exciting, they will be left with a "you-shaped" hole.

Also, make sure you don't leave behind any broken relationships or unresolved conflicts. Paul exhorts us, "If it is possible, as far as it depends on you, live at peace with everyone."[2] Do the best you can to reconcile—

---

2   Rom. 12:18. See also Matt. 5:23-24; Matt. 18:15.

if you don't you'll regret it later when distance makes communication more difficult.

As your departure date approaches, schedule times for personal renewal. Your number one priority is to keep your spiritual life intact. With all the craziness going on around you, you may find it difficult to find time to seek the Lord. Luther wisely stated that when we have no time to pray is when we most *need* to pray. Consider scheduling a mini-retreat—a few hours when you can go to a quiet, peaceful place to spend time with the Lord. If you are married, be sure to **spend more, rather than less, time with your spouse and children.** Take time to listen to one another's concerns and emotions about the move, both positive and negative, and to pray together. Focus on unity and affirmation. If you're single, find a close friend to share with and pray. Whatever you do, don't bottle up your feelings! Tears and laughter are both good medicine.

Don't be surprised if you or your family members experience sadness, or even grief, at leaving behind certain places, activities, or belongings. This is normal and natural. ***Make time to savor your favorite things one last time***, whether that means a visit to your favorite Italian restaurant, a walk in a nature reserve, or brewing steaming herb tea in your grandmother's heirloom teapot. It's especially important to help children process their sadness at leaving. Help them say good-bye to family pets, beloved toys that they can't take along, or their special playmates.

Finally, schedule in some stress-relievers. The emotional pressures of moving can take a real toll on your body. Be sure to get plenty of rest and get some outdoor exercise. Plan some relaxing activities for you and the family to "take the edge off". Rent a funny movie; go to an amusement park or the beach. Play your favorite sport. Pamper yourself at a salon. Anything that's fun *to you*!

You might want to keep this chapter handy—you'll go through many of the same emotional and physical upheaval when you leave your *adopted* nation to return to home![3]

STEP 20

GO OUT WITH JOY!

Leaving for the mission field is a big deal, so treat it like any other important occasion. Almost every culture formalizes significant life events through rites of passage: graduations, weddings, baby dedications, golden wedding anniversaries, funerals, and so on. These gatherings allow friends and family to formally witness the important occasion, and also have an outlet to express their emotions, whether joy or mourning. They strengthen the sense of community. Your departure for the mission field is an important event within your church and personal "community", so you'll want to make it a memorable occasion.

First, talk with your church leaders about a formal time of "commissioning". As we have stressed throughout the book, your church is an integral part of your ministry—you will be their "feet" on foreign soil; they are "sending" you.[4] The *kind* of ceremony you plan can be quite original, and will depend in large part on the traditions of your church: some congregations practice the laying-on-of hands; others pronounce a blessing; others offer a simple prayer. Your church may prefer to spend a few moments during the regular Sunday morning meeting, or they may

---

3   Author Neal Pirolo describes re-entry as the *most* stressful and vulnerable time for missionaries. His book *Serving as Senders* is designed to help your support team help *you*. For your own personal use, I recommend Peter Jordan's excellent book *Re-Entry: Making the Transition From Missions to Life at Home.* Jordan gives practical points for preparing to return home. Why not purchase it now so that you'll have it when you need it?

4   Rom.10:15; Acts 13:3. This spiritual act of sending does not necessarily mean that the church will be fully (or even partly) supporting the missionary with finances, although my desire would be for every church to at least participate in meeting practical needs.

choose to have a special consecration service at another time. Whatever format you and your leaders agree on, the congregation should formally witness your going-out, and understand their commitment to continue to cover you in prayer. *As the members agree in prayer for your new ministry, a spiritual blessing is imparted.*

Now celebrate! Plan an "open house" gathering for all of your friends, family, and supporters. Hopefully someone close to you has already begun organizing some festivities, but if missions is new to them, you may need to take the initiative. Whether a formal reception or a comfortable potluck (choose a style that suits your personality), the important thing is to provide a means for people to enjoy these last moments with you and your family. You've already set aside time with your intimate friends, but there are probably lots of other folks who would like to wish you well and say good-bye.

Are your bags are packed, and your tickets in hand? Congratulations! The adventure is about to begin! To help ensure that your "landing" is successful, I've shared just a few final words of advice and encouragement in the next chapters.

BEFORE MOVING ON...

Have you planned plenty of extra time in your last weeks for friends, family, and personal health?

Have you and your leaders planned an official sending ceremony at your church?

Have you provided an opportunity for your community to say good-bye to you?

LANDING ON BOTH FEET

CHAPTER ELEVEN

I finally made it! After an exhausting trip, I had arrived in my adopted country. The plane ride was just the last small step in the much longer journey of preparing to go: my church's discipleship and ministry training programs, Spanish language school, a field internship, and my own personal study of the history and culture of my new host nation. I had reached my goal at last. *Unfortunately, my excitement quickly turned to frustration, discouragement, and even tears.*

Why couldn't I understand the Spanish they spoke here? What were those strange odors? Why were the neighbors playing loud music at 3:00 in the morning? And why in the world do they have restaurants at carwashes? These were just a few of the bewildering sights, sounds, smells, and tastes that swirled around me. My first week in the Dominican Republic (now a beloved second home to me) was distressing. Despite all I had done to prepare, I felt lonely and disoriented. Nevertheless, I was determined to adapt. I privately promised myself that, whatever else I learned, I would unravel the carwash mystery.[1]

---

1 Curious? If you are from a Latin country, it's probably completely normal to you. The men enjoyed the pride of ownership of their cars (at that time, quite a luxury). What better way to enjoy their status than to relax with a beer , looking on while someone else washes the car. The ultimate? Having a beautiful woman at their side throughout.

STEP 21

___

BRACE YOURSELF FOR CULTURE SHOCK

My experience was a well-known, albeit painful, phenomenon called "culture shock"—the sense of isolation and confusion that almost always occurs when entering a new culture. If your only travel has been for shorter periods, then it's probable you've only experienced what's called the "honeymoon" stage when everything seems exciting, part of a grand adventure.[2] Those who have gone to *live* in a new culture will vouch that the honeymoon is usually followed by the sense of disorientation I described above. Only with time (and, yes, determination) will you move on to the stages of adjustment and acceptance, and even reverse culture shock upon returning home.

Can culture shock be eliminated? Probably not; but there *are* things you can to do to lessen its impact. First, learning some basic principles of cross-cultural adaptation will help you take steps to adjustment. Hopefully, part of your mission training included a module on this vital topic. If not, there are some excellent resources available. Do some personal study on your own.[3] As we discussed in depth in chapter 9, learning all you can about your host country before you arrive can cut out some unpleasant surprises (See Appendix B) and a short-term visit is worth 10,000 words! But even with the best preparation, it's highly probable that you'll go through culture shock, with the nega-

___

2   *Culture Shock USA*, by Esther Wanning, p. 232.

3   Some good general books dealing with cross-cultural adaptation are:
    From Foreign to Familiar, by Sarah Lanier (a good introduction).
    Ministering Cross-Culturally, by *Sherwood* G. Lingenfelter (a bit more technical, but quite thorough).
    Building Credible Multicultural Teams, by Lianne Roembke (includes sections on adapting to the host culture as well as working alongside team members from other cultures).
    The book *Culture Shock USA* is one of a fun series of books on about forty different countries geared to help newcomers adapt to their new surroundings. Look for one on your new country.

tive emotions (fear, confusion, anxiety, depression, and anger) often associated with it.

Culture shock is only part of an interwoven net of highly stressful life changes. Psychologists and physicians have assigned "stress factors" to a variety of life events.[4] These can include traumatic life changes, such as the death of a family member (100 points), but surprisingly include many factors that a new missionary will experience: learning a language (70), moving to a new location (40), change in financial status (38), changing to a different line of work (36 points), change in social activities (18), change in eating habits (15), and many more.[5] A total score of over 200 points indicates high risk for burnout, including being at risk for serious medical conditions. I remember taking one of these life change stress tests[6] at a team workshop. After adding in all the factors involved in cross-cultural missions, we all laughed at the fact that we should now be dead!

Decide now how you will react. There are two common reactions to the stress of cultural adaptation that are insidious to the missionary and the team: anger and withdrawal. Let's face it, when stress is piled upon stress, our negative side seems to present itself; and I guarantee there will be no lack of stress during your first months on the field! *Anger is a totally normal—but unbiblical!—response.* Often, newcomers react with frustration at their host culture: Why do the lines have

---

4   The Holmes-Rahe Stress Test was developed in 1967. There have since been a number of updates and adaptations. See *Building Credible Multicultural Teams*, p. 64-66.

5   For many new missionaries, one of the most difficult adjustments is not being in active ministry. Typically, the first phase of one's assignment is limited to language study and cultural adaptation. Most of us have been actively involved in church and outreach at home, and hate feeling like small children that can only communicate with a few babbling noises.

6   I found some interactive quizzes on the Internet. You can take one for yourself on-line. Do a search for "life change stress test".

to be so long? Why can't the workers show up on time? Why are the people so snobby? They're hypocrites, fanatics, ignoramuses, etc.—fill in the negative stereotype! Of course, it is simply a defensive reaction to everything being so *different*. Rather than trying to understand the values behind the actions, it's easy to become stuck in annoyance. In my observation, team leaders often seem to bear the brunt of anger. Of course, there's no logical reason to blow up at the leaders, but it's less painful to kick them than ourselves.

Alternatively, some missionaries withdraw into a safe and comfortable world of their own making, only occasionally sticking their toe into the water of the new culture. Typical ways to "escape" include reading books, using the internet, watching TV, or spending an excessive amount of time with folks from one's homeland. None of these are unhealthy in and of themselves; in fact, you *should* find ways to relax and seek respite from the pressures of adjusting. However, keep yourself accountable to someone so that the amount of time you spend in leisure doesn't get out of hand. In more extreme culture shock, a worker may gravitate to almost total isolation. Team members and family need to be alert for signs of depression.

"Jacob's"[7] attitude couldn't have been more self-destructive. He was so repelled by the new society that he sheltered himself in his apartment, rarely going out except for required meetings and language classes. Driven by fear, he ate only boxed cereal that he heated in the oven to kill the germs. His negative outlook was contagious, so his co-workers often avoided him. Sadly, what was needed was loving intervention: prayer, encouragement, and a heart-to-heart evaluation of his placement.

What are some **positive** ***responses to culture shock?*** First, recognize that feeling disoriented and frustrated is normal and natural. Determine to overcome your alienation, and throw in some humor to keep you

---

7   Not his real name.

smiling. Second, become a learner. Much of your shock is the natural result of not understanding the "how's" and "why's" of what is going on around you. So observe, ask questions, take notes, find a local confidant. Whenever I re-locate, I ask the Lord to give me at least one sincere friend that I can count on to explain things to me, and to honestly tell me when I'm committing a "blooper". Make creative efforts to become engaged in the society around you by exploring, making friends, and joining activities. Even if your assignment is for a few months, choose to build relationships and put down some roots.

Stay transparent and accountable to your team. Share when you are struggling, and ask for help and prayer. Although you want to limit the amount of time you spend with people from your own culture, don't eliminate it all together. You'll especially need the times of sincere Christian fellowship. Take care of yourself physically, and build in times when you can relax and be yourself, and, yes, "escape".

Finally, remember why you're there: to share the love and good news of Jesus Christ! The Apostle Paul is an excellent example of a cross-cultural minister. Wherever he traveled, he lived among the people, sharing meals with them and being a guest in their homes. He summed up his attitude by stating,

> *Though I am free and belong to no man, I make myself a slave to everyone, to win as many as possible. To the Jews I became like a Jew, to win the Jews... To those not having the law I became like one not having the law (though I am not free from God's law but am under Christ's law), so as to win those not having the law. To the weak I became weak, to win the weak.* **I have become all things to all men so that by all possible means I might save some.** *I do this all for the sake of the gospel, that I may share in its blessings. (1 Cor. 9:19-23. Emphasis mine)*

As you lean on the Holy Spirit, He is able to help you love the seemingly unlovely, and to give you sufficient grace for every situation.

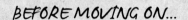

BEFORE MOVING ON...

Have you studied the principles of cross-cultural adaptation?

Have you researched some of the cultural values and mores of your new society?

Have you chosen in advance to respond Biblically to culture shock?

Have you established an accountability system with someone in your new location?

STAYING THE COURSE

AN EPILOGUE

We began our walk together with some rather somber statistics: one third of all those heading into missions do not complete their first term on the field.[1] But as the writer of Hebrews said, "Even though we speak like this, dear friends, we are confident of better things in your case."[2] Through your diligent preparation and prayer, you have eliminated many of the factors leading to missionary attrition. You are as equipped as you reasonably can be to embark on your new venture, and the Lord is at your side.

Even so, you will have to fiercely resist the devil. Most of us are familiar with Paul's famous passage on the armor of God. But have you ever noted what he states is our goal? When the battle dust has settled, we want to be able to proclaim, "I stood my ground!"

> *Finally, be strong in the Lord and in His might power. Put on the full armor of God so that you can **take your stand against the devil's schemes** ... Therefore, put on the full armor of God so that when the day of evil comes, you may be able to **stand your ground**, and after you have done everything, to **stand**. **Stand firm**, then. (Eph. 6: 10-11, 13-1. Emphasis mine.)*

What, then, are the characteristics that will make for long-term fruitfulness on the field? There are many factors that will help you

---

1   Taylor, p. 125.

2   Heb. 6:9.

continue to bear fruit on the field: flexibility, good health, adequate financial support, on-going training, healthy family relationships ... the list could go on and on. But as I reflect on my own years in missions, I would like to leave you with a few life habits that will help sustain you through the many storms of life on the field.

First, cultivate intimacy with God. God has been my closest friend, my brother, my father, and my husband through the lonely and dark hours of my life, as well as in the mountaintop times. He has comforted me in betrayals, sat beside my sickbed, kept me company when I was left alone, and given me wisdom in thorny situations. He has shared my triumphs, been right there with me on fun, new adventures, and even enjoyed a chuckle with me when life got ridiculous. Am I super-spiritual? Definitely not. God is super-good! He and I both know that I would never have made it without His friendship. The mission field will offer you opportunities for a far deeper relationship with the Lord than you ever dreamed possible!

But intimacy *does* have to be cultivated. ***Developing regular personal disciplines of prayer, worship, and Bible study is essential to your well-being on the field.*** Even if you are part of a healthy team, you will probably not have the kind of teaching, fellowship, and corporate worship that you are used to at home. No matter how busy things get, make your personal devotional life your highest priority.

Second, keep yourself transparent and accountable to your leaders. I have a spiritual safety rule that has kept me from going over a few cliffs. I've made a life-long promise to myself that I will talk to my leaders (or a trustworthy accountability partner) about any struggles I am going through. To bring it down to earth, my rule is, if there's something I want to hide, then I know I need to talk about it. Oh, yes, it can be embarrassing. None of us likes for people to know about our hidden "issues". But as we confess our sins to each other and pray for one another, we—and our thought life—come into the light, and the enemy is put to flight.[3]

Along these same lines, ***listen and respond to the counsel you receive from your leaders and those who love you.*** Over the years, a number of godly men and women have lovingly instructed, corrected, and yes, rebuked me, all for my personal growth in godliness. On a few occasions, I received wrong counsel. In two cases, I was wrongly disciplined when false accusations were made against me. I know that the Lord worked for good in each of these situations, as I humbled myself and honored the Lord through my submission. But nine times out of ten, the instruction and correction I have received has been right on the mark, helping me to grow and change, and keeping me from Satan's snares.

Finally, ***treasure your friends and supporters.*** They will be your encouraging crowd of witnesses,[4] cheering you on as you run the race, and helping you get back up when you stumble. Keep communication lines open, and take time to invest in relationships. ***In a nutshell, the key to staying the course is relationship: first with God, and then with those He has placed around you.***

Thank you for so patiently allowing me to be a part of your journey. I hope someday to hear of your adventures in missions and of the ways that God is working in you and through you. Now as you continue on your way, please permit me to pray for you:

> *May you go out with joy and be led forth with peace;*
> *May the mountains and the hills burst into song before you.*
> *(Is. 55:12)*

> *May the Lord bless you and keep you;*
> *May the Lord make His face shine upon you and be gracious to you.*
> *(Num. 6:25)*

---

3 James 5:16.

4 Heb. 12:1.

A NOTE

You have been entrusted with a special treasure: your missionaries! Hopefully, as you have read this book, you have grasped the importance of the church becoming an integral part of sending process. You've counseled, you've prayed, you've encouraged, and at last they are on their way. It's been a big job to do it right, but you've helped to get them on the field; you breathe a sigh of relief. But it's not time to take your rest—*your job is just beginning!* Launching a new missionary is much like giving birth to a baby. The most intense part is over, but there is still a lot of work to be done to ensure for their care and growth. And, like infants, your workers will be extremely vulnerable during the challenges of their first few months on the field.

My dear friend Ken[1], a dear friend and a national leader for his mission, had poured enormous time and resources into launching the first long-term team from that country to the 10/40 Window. He thought that once they arrived at their destination he would be able to return his focus to his many other responsibilities. He soon learned that his involvement, while gradually diminishing, was imperative. There were pastoral concerns, financial issues, practical and administrative matters, and a few full-out crises, all of which required his attention.

It is ironic that your workers' distance from home makes your pastoral care more challenging just as it becomes more crucially needed. They

---

1   Not his real name.

have joined the front lines of spiritual warfare, yet are geographically cut off from the rest of the church body. Communication difficulties can often make them feel emotionally and spiritually cut off, as well. They will probably face physical hardships, culture shock, spiritual pressures, and possibly be under financial stress, as well.

So what are the roles of the pastor and the home church? First and foremost, you must ensure that your missionaries are blanketed in prayer—not only yours, but by the congregation as a whole. Ensure that they feel loved and cared for through regular and creative communication, including encouragement and news from home. You will need to continue to pastor them in their emotional and spiritual struggles. This will mean periodically checking in with deeper questioning than, "How are you doing?" You will also need to check on their physical health and safety. Whether or not your church is the primary source of finances for your missionaries, you will need to be sure that your missionary's basic needs are being met.[2] In some cases, you may need to intervene with a pastoral visit or even call them home.

Obviously, this kind of support is not a one-man job. Perhaps others on the church staff or leadership will play a part in the pastoral care your missionaries. Maybe you will choose to form a mission committee to handle many of the more practical matters. As you put into place the needed structures for the on-going care of those on the field, consider six areas of support:[3]

- Pastoral care, encouragement, and moral support.

- Logistics support (practical and administrative concerns).

---

2   Remember that a leading cause for missionaries returning home is inadequate support. ("Missionary Attrition: The ReMAP Research Report", Peter W. Brierley, in Taylor, p. 94.)

3   Adapted from *Serving as Senders*, by Neal Pirolo. I highly recommend this book as a guide for caring for your missionaries.

- Financial support.

- Prayer support.

- Communication support (both to and from the missionary).

- Re-entry support.[4]

If you and your church are new at this, there are plenty of good resources available to get you started.[5] Don't be embarrassed to ask for help. If your missionaries are affiliated with agency, get for their input. Meet with leaders of churches that have successfully sustained their missionaries over a long period of time. Glean principles and techniques that have worked for them. As you put missions at the heart of your church, God will be sure to bring a blessing. After all, you are doing that which is most dear to *His* heart. **May God bless you as you shepherd those that God has entrusted to your care!**

---

4 Surprisingly, returning home can be just as stressful, or more, than *going* to the field. See chapters 1 and 7 in Pirolo.

5 Some helpful websites with related links are:
www.missionaryresources.org;
www.missionarycare.com;
www.membercare.org.

A PARTIAL LIST OF SCRIPTURES RELATING TO MISSIONS[1]

APPENDIX A

Old Testament and missions

- Genesis 12:1-3 (repeated in Gen. 18:18, 22:17-18, 26:24 and 28:12-14)
- Exodus 9:14-16 – purpose of the plagues
- Exodus 19:6 – Israel was to be a "kingdom of priests"
- Numbers 14:21 – glory of Lord fills the whole earth
- Deuteronomy 4:6-8 – show your understanding to the nations
- Deuteronomy 10:19 – "You are to love those who are aliens"
- Deuteronomy 28:10 – "all the peoples on the earth will see that you are called by the name of the Lord"
- Deuteronomy 32:1 - "Hear, O earth, the words of my mouth."
- Joshua 4:24 – "so that all the peoples of the earth might know"
- 1 Samuel 2:10 – "The LORD will judge the ends of the earth."

1   Taken from Southern Nazarene University's excellent website. http://home.snu.edu/~hculbert/biblical.htm.

- 1 Samuel 17:46 – "the whole world will know there is a God in Israel"

- 1 Kings 8:41-43, 59-60 (also in 2 Chronicles 6:32-33) – "so that all peoples of the earth may know your name" (Solomon's prayer at dedication of Temple)

- 2 Kings 19:15 – "Hezekiah prayed ... : O LORD, you alone are God over all the kingdoms of the earth.'"

- 1 Chronicles 16:31 "Let the earth be glad; let them say among the nations, The Lord reigns!'"

- 1 Chronicles 16:24 – "Declare his glory among the nations, his marvelous deeds among all peoples"

- 2 Chronicles 6:33 – "so that all the peoples of the earth may know your name and fear you"

- Psalm 2:7-10 – "You are my Son ... I will make the nations your inheritance"

- Psalm 7:7-8 – "Let the Lord judge the peoples"

- Psalm 8:9 – "How majestic is your name in all the earth!"

- Psalm 18:49 – "I will praise you among the nations"

- Psalm 22:26-28 – "all the families of the nations will bow down"

- Psalm 19:1-4 – "their words to the ends of the world"

- Psalm 22:27 – "All the ends of the earth will remember and turn to the Lord"

- Psalm 24 – "The earth is the Lord's"

- Psalm 33 – "Blessed is the nation whose God is the Lord"

- Psalm 45:17 – "The nations will praise you for ever and ever"

- Psalm 46:10 – "I will be exalted among the nations"

- Psalm 47 – "God reigns over the nations"
- Psalm 48:10 – "Like your name, O God, your praise reaches to the ends of the earth"
- Psalm 49:1 – "Hear this, all you peoples; listen, all who live in this world"
- Psalm 50 – "From the rising of the sun to the place where it sets"
- Psalm 57 – "I will sing of you among the peoples"
- Psalm 59:13 – "It will be known to the ends of the earth that God rules over Jacob."
- Psalm 65:5-8 – "the hope of all the ends of the earth ... where morning dawns and evening fades you call forth songs of joy"
- Psalm 66 – "All the earth bows down to you ... Praise our God, O peoples"
- Psalm 67 – "your salvation among all peoples"
- Psalm 68:32 – "Sing to God, O kingdoms of the earth"
- Psalm 72 – "all nations will serve him"
- Psalm 72:9 – "the desert tribes will bow before him"
- Psalm 72:17, 19 – "All nations will be blessed through him ... May the whole earth be filled with his glory"
- Psalm 77:14 – "you display your power among the peoples"
- Psalm 82 – "all the nations are your inheritance"
- Psalm 83:18 – "You alone are the Most High over all the earth."
- Psalm 86:8-13 – all nations will come and worship
- Psalm 87 – the register of the peoples

- Psalm 96 – "sing to the Lord, all the earth ... Declare his glory among the nations"

- Psalm 97 – "The Lord reigns, let the earth be glad; let the distant shores rejoice"

- Psalm 98:3 – "All the ends of the earth have seen the salvation of our God."

- Psalm 98:9 – "He comes to judge the earth. He will judge the world in righteousness and the peoples with equity."

- Psalm 99:1-3 – "He is exalted over all the nations. Let them praise your great and awesome name"

- Psalm 102:15 – "The nations will fear the name of the LORD, all the kings of the earth will revere your glory."

- Psalm 102:22 – "when the peoples and the kingdoms assemble to worship the Lord"

- Psalm 105:1 – "make known among the nations what He has done"

- Psalm 106:8 – reason for dividing the Red Sea

- Psalm 108:3 – "I will sing of you among the peoples"

- Psalm 108:5 – "Be exalted, O God, above the heavens, and let your glory be over all the earth."

- Psalm 110:6 – "He will judge the nations,"

- Psalm 113:3 – "From the rising of the sun to the place where it sets, the name of the Lord is to be praised"

- Psalm 117 – "Praise the Lord, all you nations"

- Psalm 126 – "it was said among the nations"

- Psalm 135 – "our Lord is greater than all gods"

- Psalm 138:4 – "may all the kings of the earth praise you, O Lord"

- Isaiah 2:3 – "Many peoples will come and say, "Come, let us go up to the mountain of the Lord, to the house of the God of Jacob.

- Isaiah 6:3 – "They were calling to one another: Holy, holy, holy is the Lord Almighty; the whole earth is full of his glory.'"

- Isaiah 11:9 – "fill the earth with the knowledge of the Lord"

- Isaiah 11:10 – "in that day a Root of Jesse will stand as a banner for the peoples, the nations ..."

- Isaiah 12:4 – "Make known among the nations what He has done"

- Isaiah 24:16 – "From the ends of the earth we hear singing: Glory to the Righteous One.'"

- Isaiah 25:6 – "the LORD Almighty will prepare a feast of rich food for all peoples"

- Isaiah 42:4 – "in His law the islands will put their hope"

- Isaiah 42:6 – "I will keep you and will make you to be a covenant for the people and a light for the Gentiles."

- Isaiah 34:1 – "Come near, you nations, and listen; pay attention, you peoples!"

- Isaiah 37:16 – "O Lord Almighty ... , you alone are God over all the kingdoms of the earth."

- Isaiah 42:4 – "He will not falter or be discouraged till he establishes justice on earth. In his law the islands will put their hope."

- Isaiah 43:6 – "I will say to the north, 'Give them up!' and to the south, 'Do not hold them back.'"

- Isaiah 45:6 – "from the rising of the sun to the place of its setting men may know there is none besides me."

- Isaiah 45:22 – "Turn to me ... all you ends of the earth"

- Isaiah 49:1-6 – "I will make you a light for the Gentiles"

- Isaiah 49:22 – "The Sovereign Lord says: "See, I will beckon to the Gentiles, I will lift up my banner to the peoples.""

- Isaiah 52:10 – "The Lord will lay bare his holy arm in the sight of all the nations, and all the ends of the earth will see the salvation of our God."

- Isaiah 56:7 – "my house shall be called a house of prayer for all nations"

- Isaiah 59:19 – "From the west, men will fear the name of the Lord, and from the rising of the sun, they will revere His glory."

- Isaiah 60:3 – "Nations will come to your light"

- Isaiah 62:11 – "The Lord has made proclamation to the ends of the earth"

- Isaiah 66:19 – "They will proclaim my glory among the nations"

- Jeremiah 3:17 – "All nations will gather in Jerusalem to honor the name of the Lord"

- Jeremiah 16:19 To you the nations will come from the ends of the earth and say, "Our fathers possessed nothing but false gods, worthless idols that did them no good."

- Ezekiel 36:22-23 – "The nations will know I am the Lord"

- Daniel 2:47; 4:1-2; 6:25 – "Surely your God is the God of gods"

- Daniel 7:13, 14 – "all peoples, nations and languages should serve Him"

- Jonah's story – the missionary book of the Old Testament [e-book on Jonah]
- Micah 1:2 – "Hear, O peoples, all of you, listen, O earth and all who are in it."
- Micah 4:2 – "Many nations will come"
- Micah 5:4 – "His greatness will reach to the ends of the earth."
- Habbakuk 2:14 – "The earth will be filled with the knowledge of the glory of the Lord, as the water cover the sea"
- Zephaniah 2:11 – "Nations on every shore will worship him"
- Zephaniah 3:9 – "Then will I purify the lips of the peoples, that all of them may call on the name of the Lord."
- Haggai 2:7 – "Desire of all nations"
- Zechariah 2:11 – "Many nations will be joined with the Lord in that day and will become my people"
- Zechariah 8:20-23 – "Many peoples and inhabitants of many cities will come"
- Zechariah 9:10 – "He will proclaim peace to the nations"
- Zechariah 14:9 – "The Lord will be king over the whole earth."
- Malachi 1:10-11 – "My name will be great among the nations, from the rising to the setting of the sun"

New Testament and missions

- Matthew 4:8-11 – Temptation of Jesus
- Matthew 6:9-10 – The Lord's prayer

- Matthew 10:18 – "On my account you will be brought before governors and kings as witnesses to them and to the Gentiles."

- Matthew 13 (Ezekiel 17:23) – parables of sower, weeds, mustard seed, fishing net

- Matthew 24:14 – the gospel will be preached in the whole world

- Matthew 28:19-20; Mark 16:15 - The Great Commission *(which many say is a re-statement of God's promise to Abraham in Genesis 12)* [Rev. Susan Fitkin's reflection on the passage]

- Mark 11:17 (Isaiah 56:7) – a house of prayer for all nations

- Mark 13:10 – "the gospel must first be preached to all nations"

- Mark 16:15 (see Matthew 28:19-20)

- Luke 2:32 – "a light for revelation to the Gentiles"

- Luke 10:2 – "harvest is plentiful, but the workers are few"

- Luke 10:27 – "love your neighbor as yourself"

- John 3:16 [text of verse]

- John 12:32 – "I, when I am lifted up from the earth, will draw all men to myself."

- John 21:4-14 – some Biblical commentators have said the 153 fish equals the number of all the tribes and nations which the ancients thought existed on earth

- Acts 1:8; 2:5-12 13:47 (Isaiah 49:6) – witnesses in all the earth

- Acts 3:25 – "He said to Abraham, Through your offspring, all peoples on earth will be blessed.'"

- Acts 9:15 "Go! This man is my chosen instrument to carry my name before the Gentiles and their kings."

- Acts 11:18 – "They praised God, saying, So then, God has granted even the Gentiles repentance unto life.'"

- Acts 13:47 – "I have made you a light for the Gentiles, that you may bring salvation to the ends of the earth." (Isaiah 49:6)

- Acts 14:27 – "They reported all that God had done through them and how he had opened the door of faith to the Gentiles."

- Acts 28:28 – "Therefore I want you to know that God's salvation has been sent to the Gentiles, and they will listen!"

- Romans 1:5 – "We received grace and apostleship to call people from among all the Gentiles to obedience."

- Romans 3:29 – "Is God the God of Jews only? Is he not the God of Gentiles too? Yes, of Gentiles too."

- Romans 10:12-15 – "How can they hear?"

- Romans 15:10 "Rejoice, O Gentiles, with his people." (Deuteronomy 32:43]

- Romans 15:11 "Praise the Lord, all you Gentiles, and sing praises to him, all you peoples." (Psalm 117:1)

- Romans 16:26 – So that all nations might believe

- 2 Corinthians 4:15 – "grace that is reaching more and more people"

- Galatians 3:8 – "The Scripture foresaw that God would justify the Gentiles by faith, and announced the gospel in advance to Abraham: All nations will be blessed through you.'" (Genesis 12:3; 18:18; 22:18)

- Galatians 3:14 – "He redeemed us in order that the blessing given to Abraham might come to the Gentiles."

- Ephesians 1:10 – "To bring all things in heaven and on earth together under one head, even Christ."

- Ephesians 2:11-19 – "you are no longer foreigners and aliens"

- Philippians 2:10 – Every knee shall bow

- 1 Thessalonians 2:15-16 – "to keep us from speaking to the Gentiles so that they may be saved"

- Hebrews 6:13-14 – God's promise to Abraham

- 2 Peter 3:9, 12 – "not wanting anyone to perish"

- 1 John 2:2 – "He is the atoning sacrifice ... for the sins of the whole world"

- Revelation 5:9 – "you purchased men for God from every tribe and language and people and nation"

- Revelation 7:9 – Every tribe, tongue, people and nation

- Revelation 14:6 – "The angel had the eternal gospel to proclaim to those who live on the earth – to every nation, tribe, language and people."

- Revelation 15:4 – "all nations will come and worship before you"

- Revelation 21:23-24 – "The Lamb is its lamp. The nations will walk by its light"

COUNTRY RESEARCH QUESTIONS

APPENDIX B

Information on the following areas will give you insight into the people and the spiritual climate, and help you prepare your strategies:[1]

- ☐ Geography

- ☐ Population, ethnic groups, language(s)

- ☐ History

- ☐ Political system

- ☐ Economy and wealth/poverty

- ☐ Communication and transportation infrastructures

- ☐ Religion(s)

- ☐ Christian work, response to the Gospel, and number of believers

- ☐ Literacy and Education

- ☐ Nutrition, health and medical care

---

1   *Operation World* provides a brief summary for many of these items. In addition, informational websites are listed by country in Appendix 2. The Joshua Project also has information grouped by both country and people group, along with related links. Take time to explore their website: http://www.joshuaproject.net. A simple "google" search will give you plenty of information to mine.

- [ ] Societal structure (tribes, castes, class systems, etc.)

- [ ] Cultural aspects[2] (housing, dress, food, marriage and divorce, family structure, interaction between the sexes, attitudes about aging, attitudes about time, ways of resolving conflict, relationship with the West, music and art, sports and recreation, important values, belief structures, taboos, etc.)

---

2   *From Foreign to Familiar* (Lanier) is a good introduction to the types of internalized values that can cause culture shock and misunderstandings. *Ministering Cross-Culturally* (Lingenfelter) and *Building Multicultural Teams* (Roembke) provide a more in-depth study of societal structures and values, with questionnaires to assess your home and your target culture.

PRE-TRAVEL INFORMATION CHECKLIST

APPENDIX C

To help plan your trip, you'll want to carefully research all of the following areas well before your departure date.[1]

- ☐ What are the legal entry requirements? Do you need a passport? Visa? Residency papers? Work permit? What is the best method to obtain the documents you need? What is the maximum length of stay permitted on the kind of visa you will have? Are missionaries allowed, or will you enter as a "tentmaker", a tourist, or an aid worker?

- ☐ What is the best way to arrive? Be sure to check with those who travel regularly to the area before making your reservations. Ask your team to recommend a travel agent if you are traveling to a region where certain airlines should be avoided, or for which tickets are not available online.

- ☐ Check on weight and baggage limits for each leg of your journey. Generally, flights within a continent have tighter restrictions. Is there a way to appeal for a higher weight limit?

---

1   Rather than give a long list of web resources, I will simply point you to Emercy's website: www.missionaryresources.org. It offers information and links on most of the items listed above. If you are not comfortable "surfing the net", they have a print version available. You can e-mail them at info@emercy.org. You may also wish to use travel guides such as the *Let's Go* or *Lonely Planet* series to get information on travel, weather, transportation, etc.

☐ Find out the local currency and the exchange rate with your own. Has it been fluctuating? Get as good an estimate as possible so that you can properly plan your budget. Should you change money before arriving? Which currency will get you the best exchange rate (Euros, dollars, etc.?), and is it possible to exchange your own currency there? Will you be able to make bank transfers there and/or cash checks? Will you be able to use your credit cards or withdraw cash from an ATM? How much cash should you carry?

☐ If you have not done so already, be sure to get the information you need to prepare a detailed budget that will include travel expenses, living expenses in your new locale, as well as an emergency fund.

☐ Will the team be preparing your housing for you? What will the cost be? How will you furnish it? Are there items you'll want to ship from home? If so, what's the best method?

☐ What kind of local transportation is available? Is there a team vehicle? Public transportation? Or will you need to plan for the purchase of a vehicle?

☐ If you will be studying the language at your field locale, what are your options for classes or tutoring? How much will it cost? What kind of study materials should you take (tape player, dictionary, etc.)?

☐ What are the communication outlets, and what are the costs? Ask about e-mail and internet, telephones and cell phones, faxes, mail, receiving packages, etc. By the way, don't forget the obvious—how much time difference is there between your home country and your destination? Be sure to remind your family and friends, or you may get 4:00 am phone calls!

☐ Both electrical and phone connections may be different. Is the voltage is 110 or 220, or if you will even *have* regular power! If the electricity is unreliable, you may need a voltage regulator, battery back-up for your computer, flashlights, etc. Research exactly what kind of adaptors and/or transformers will you need.[2] Phone jacks may also differ from country to country, so you may need to look for an adaptor for your computer modem.

☐ Be sure to find out about security issues and communication guidelines if you are going to either a restricted access nation or a politically sensitive area. Is e-mail encryption or some other form of secure communication recommended? What are things you can and can't say in letters, e-mails, phone conversations? What should you inform people who will be writing or calling you? What are some topics you can or can't speak about in public? ***Be sure to respect your team's guidelines!*** Your carelessness can place others in danger, especially local believers.

☐ Learn as much as you can about cultural "do's and don'ts", particularly any taboos that could cause serious offense. Find out about greetings and hospitality (giving and receiving); rules about interactions between males and females, young and old; topics of conversation considered inappropriate; courtesies and modest behavior; and so on.

☐ Learn as much as you can about the religious practices and beliefs within the culture. If you will be working among Christians, learn about their special customs (greetings,

---

2   Note that if you will be changing from 110V to 220V, or vice versa, heat-generating items such as irons, coffee makers or hair dryers require large and heavy transformers. Look for travel appliances that can be used with either 110 or 220V, or make your purchase when you arrive.

dress, etc.). If you will be working in a non-Christian environment, find out how much liberty you will have to share your faith openly and whether or not there is an expatriate church for foreign visitors.

- ☐ Ask what kind of clothing, including footwear, you will need. Appropriate cultural guidelines should apply for age and gender, but you'll also want to know what will be comfortable in the climate for both your daily routines and special occasions. Also learn what you can purchase there, and what you will need to buy at home.

- ☐ If you have children, you'll obviously want to know what educational options are open to you: public, private, mission or home school.

- ☐ Ask about health issues. Will you need any vaccinations before going? Can you obtain quality prescription medications there, or should you take your own? Is good medical care available, or do you need evacuation insurance? If you or a family member has a chronic health condition or allergy, learn what precautions and preparations you will need to make.

- ☐ Learn about food and drinking water. What is the typical diet there? Will you be able to find the foods you are more accustomed to? Are your favorite seasonings and ingredients available locally? And what about that favorite "something" (mine is coffee) that you want to be sure to have on hand? Are vitamins recommended? A professional quality water filter?

- ☐ Ask the team to help you think of personal items that will be helpful to have—but difficult to purchase. Some items to consider are: first aid kits, bedding and towels, office products, toiletries, and items for recreation and relaxation. The silliest things become quite valuable when it's impossible to get them: a can opener, safety pins, camera batteries, zip-lock bags, books, and, yes, toilet paper! Depending on the cultural distance from your home country and the geographical remoteness, the list can be long and amusing. Find out if you should you take gifts to give out to nationals. Is there some special item that you can bless the team members with? You should also ask them if there are some things you *shouldn't* bring—a patriotic t-shirt, an offensive book, items that would be easily damaged or that won't function there, etc.

☐ Hopefully, when you researched your team, you asked about team policies. If you haven't already done so, be sure to do so now. Ask about your daily and weekly schedule, length of service commitment, vacations, fees, etc., etc.

You will undoubtedly think of even *more* questions. If you do, please write so that I can add them to my list!

PREPARING YOUR FAMILY'S BUDGET[1]

APPENDIX D

BUDGET WORKSHEET
PART I:
One-time Relocation Expenses

Instructions: Research how much you will need for each of the following items:

Airfare and other travel expenses
(include cost of passports and visas)

Vehicle (if you will be
purchasing one)

Furnishing and equipping your new
home and/or shipping costs

---

1   These worksheets are for your initial planning. Once on the field, you will need to develop a simple spreadsheet to keep track of both income and spending. Monthly tracking serves several purposes. 1) As you write down your expenditures, you will see each month if you are going over budget, and where you may need to cut back. 2) At the end of the year you will be able to re-evaluate your budget and plan more accurately for future expenses. 3) You will be able to give an account to your leaders of how you spend your money. 4) Your tracking may help future missionaries plan *their* budgets. 5) Finally, recording your sources of income, including individual donors, will keep you from forgetting to recognize a supporter. (*Friend Raising* has some helpful forms in the appendices for keeping track of donations, as well as a budget worksheet.) If you need help, find someone on your support team who is gifted in accounting and ask for assistance.

Up-front purchase of necessary
items (equipment, luggage,
clothing, medical, ministry
materials, etc.)

Other: (specify)

TOTAL ONE-TIME
RELOCATION EXPENSES:

Available start-up cash:

Special gifts

Savings or special funds

Sale of home or vehicle

Sale of stocks or bonds

Other:

TOTAL START-UP CASH
AVAILABLE:

Funds still needed:
(Expenses less available cash)

BUDGET WORKSHEET
PART II:
Estimated Monthly Field Expenses

Tithes and offerings[2]

Housing and utilities

Food

Miscellaneous household expenses

Communication (postage, internet, phone, etc.)

Books, office, supplies, etc.

Clothing

Education (include language lessons)

Transportation and/or vehicle expenses

Medical and other insurance

Medical and dental expenses

Ministry expenses

---

2   Many a missionary has gotten into financial hot water by neglecting to tithe. Even the Levites, the Old Testament equivalent of full-time workers, were required to tithe. (See Num. 18:25-30; Mal. 3:8-10; Heb. 7:4-10.)

Gifts and hospitality[3]

Conferences and travel[4]

Recreation and vacation

Personal/miscellaneous

Taxes[5] (federal, state,
social security)

Savings and emergency fund[6]

Debt payments[7]

Other: (specify)

TOTAL MONTHLY EXPENSES:

AVAILABLE MONTHLY INCOME:

---

3   Gifts and hospitality may be important ministry expenditures in your culture. Find out!

4   How often will you leave the town? The country? How often will you return to your home country? What are the costs of conferences? Calculate the total annual costs and divide by 12 for an estimated monthly expense.

5   Find out *before* you go what kind of taxes you will need to pay in both your home country and your host country. If taxes will not be deducted automatically from your paycheck, you will probably need to budget for a significant amount.

6   If you are going to be in missions long-term, you will need to budget for children's college expenses, retirement, and so on, in addition to building an emergency fund.

7   Obviously, you will want to do all you can to eliminate debt before going to the field, particularly the burden of high interest credit card debt. However, some student loans may be manageable, or you may even find a program that will pay off your loans in exchange for working in a needy area.

Monthly pledges/missions/
denominational support

Monthly income from work or
other sources

One time offerings (divided by
number of months on the field)

TOTAL MONTHLY INCOME:

Funds still needed:
(Expenses less available cash)

SELECTED BIBLIOGRAPHY

Adopt-a-People Clearinghouse. http://www.adoptapeople.com.

Bruchko. Bruce Olson, Creation House, Orlando, FL, USA, 1995.

Building Credible Multicultural Teams. Lianne Roembke, William Carey Library, Pasadena, CA, USA, 2000.

Celebration of Discipline: The Path to Spiritual Growth, 20ᵗʰ Anniversary Edition. Richard J. Foster. HarperCollins Publishers, San Francisco, CA, USA, 1998.

The Church is Bigger than You Think: Structures and Strategies for the Church in the 21ˢᵗ Century. Patrick Johnstone, William Carey Library, Pasadena, CA, USA, 1998.

Esperanza para los Musulmanes. Don McCurry, Unilit.

Establishing Ministry Training: A Manual for Programme Developers. Edited by Dr. Robert W. Ferris, William Carey Library, Pasadena, CA, USA, 1995.

Foreign to Familiar: A Guide to Understanding Hot- and Cold-Climate Culture. Sarah A. Lanier; McDougal Publishing, Hagerstown, MD, USA, 2000.

Friend-Raising: Building a Missionary Support Team that Lasts. Second Edition. Betty Barnett, YWAM Publishing, Seattle, WA, USA, 2003.

Getting Sent: A Relational Approach to Support Raising. Pete Sommer; InterVarsity Press, Downers Grove, IL, USA, 1999.

Getting There from Here: How to Find Your Place in God's Global Picture, Revised Edition. Elizabeth Goldsmith; OM Publishing, Carlisle, Cumbria, UK, 1995.

Healing the Broken Family of Abraham: A New Life for Muslims. Don McCurry. Ministries to Muslims. Colorado Springs, CO, USA, 2001.

Honorably Wounded. Marjorie F. Foyle, MARC Europe, Bromley, Kent, UK, 1987.

Is That Really You, God? Hearing the Voice of God. Loren Cunningham with Janice Rogers, Chosen Books of the Zondervan Corporation, Grand Rapids, MI, USA, 1984.

The Joshua Project, http://www.joshuaproject.net.

Ministering Cross-Culturally: An Incarnational Model for Personal Relationships. Sherwood G. Lingenfelter and Marvin K. Mayers, Baker Book House Company, USA, 1986.

The Missionary Resources Handbook, 3rd Edition. The print version of www. Missionaryresources.org, a project of Emercy.

"A Partial Listing of Scriptures Relating to Missions". http://home.snu.edu/~hculbert/ biblical.htm (Southern Nazarene University).

Perspectives Exposure: Discovering God's Heart for All Nations and Our Part in His Plan. Edited by Meg Crossman; YWAM Publishing, Seattle, WA, USA, 2003.

Perspectives on the World Christian Movement: A Reader. Third Edition. Edited by Ralph D. Winter and Steven C. Hawthorne; William Carey Library, Pasadena, CA, USA, 1999.

Perspectives on the World Christian Movement: The Notebook. 1999 Edition. . Edited by Ralph D. Winter and Steven C. Hawthorne; William Carey Library, Pasadena, CA, USA, 1999.

Re-Entry: Making the Transition From Missions to Life at Home. Peter Jordan, YWAM Publishing, Seattle, WA, USA,.

Send Me! Your Journey to the Nations. Steve Hoke and Bill Taylor; World Evangelical Fellowship Commission and William Carey Library, Pasadena, CA, USA, 1999.

Serving as Senders. Neal Pirolo, Emmaus Road International, Emmaus Road International, San Diego, CA, USA, 1991.

Spiritual Warfare for Every Christian. Dean Sherman with Bill Payne. YWAM Publishing, Seattle, WA, USA, 1990.

A Tale of Three Kings: A Study in Brokenness. Gene Edwards, Tyndale House Publishers, Inc., Wheaton, IL, USA, 1980.

Understanding Latin Americans. Eugene A. Nida; Willliam Carey Library, Pasadena, CA, USA, 1974.

Your Mission, Should You Accept It.... An Introduction for World Christians. Stephen Gaukroger; InterVarsity Press, Downers Grove, IL, USA, 1996.

INDEX

Timothy, 67
training, iii, v, cii, 38-41, 48-49, 53, 61-63, 65-66, 71, 85, 109
    components, 63-64, 71
    formal. *See* Internship
    model, 59-62
    specialized, 57, 61
    technical, 65
        training theory, 61

U

Urbana Student Missions Conference, 50

W

Winter, Ralph, 4
World War II, 87
Wycliffe Bible Translators, 32, 47

Y

YWAM, 11, 32, 47, 57, 74, 82
    School of Frontier Missions, 74